HOW TO ENJOY BALLET

Mary Clarke and Clement Crisp

Series Editor Melvyn Bragg

PIATKUS

To Dame Alicia Markova,
great dancer, great teacher,
great friend

———————

© 1983 Mary Clarke and Clement Crisp

First published in 1983 by Judy Piatkus (Publishers) Limited,
5 Windmill Street, London W1
This paperback edition first published in 1987

British Library Cataloguing in Publication Data

Crisp, Clement
How to enjoy ballet.——(Melvyn Bragg's arts series)
1. Ballet
I. Title   II. Clarke, Mary, *1923–*
792.8   GV1787
ISBN 0-86188-604-6

Designed by Zena Flax

Typeset by Phoenix Photosetting, Chatham, Kent
Printed and bound in Great Britain by
Mackays of Chatham Ltd

Frontispiece: Natalia Makarova as Aurora in *The Sleeping Beauty*

contents

Mikhail Baryshnikov in Twyla Tharp's *Push Comes to Shove*.

introduction

Almost everybody dances, even if they dance alone. Social occasions can make dancing an insupportable strain for the socially nervous. Lack of technique can paralyse desire. But everybody wants to dance, especially in celebration. Ballet celebrates the act of dancing itself. Because of its historical development it has, until recently, been out of reach of the widest public. This has led to prejudices and myths which are founded only in ignorance: the myth, for example, that male dancers are 'soft' when in fact they are tough, athletic and astoundingly strong; the prejudice, for example, that ballet can only be understood and even practised by the very few – a prejudice which simply dissolves when exposed to touring companies, encouragement and education at school and through television. Ballet has seen the biggest boom in the performing arts over the last 25 years, and it shows not the slightest sign of abating.

This book should provide both a stimulus and a support. It is thorough, incisive and authoritative, as is to be expected from the two authors. They manage to range over the history of ballet without being either too detailed or at all superficial; they are practical, providing a glossary, summaries of plots, and fundamental information about ballet techniques; but above all they are passionately committed to the ballet. Even if you begin to read this book in a sceptical state of mind, I believe you will stay to praise. For those who have an interest in ballet which, for one reason or another, they may not have been able to cultivate – lack of opportunity, shyness, a feeling of having 'missed out' or it being 'too late' or 'not for them' – this book is a comprehensive, enthusiastic and most conscientious introduction. The authors care about the subject so much that they want others to care; their verve is infectious. I would suggest that even those who know something – or, indeed, almost everything – about ballet will find in this succinct volume a most useful and entertaining survey and handbook. To write well without writing down, to write for the well-informed and at the same time reach out to those who, starting almost from scratch, wish to be well-informed is a difficult and underestimated talent. Like all talents of a high order it has to be supported by massive hard work. The learning here, though displayed with a light almost lyrical touch, is very well founded. The talent to communicate will, I trust, be self-proving.

Like most people of my generation – the pre-TV-in-childhood generation – I was brought up with ballet as distant a prospect as Atlantis. There were no ballet companies within a hundred miles of where I lived; no touring company visited the town or the school; above all, no television brought great performers and star productions into the home. I loved dancing yet Ballet was something I saw referred to in books or caught in a film, a one or two-minute extract; it was a tempting foreign country.

Without realising it, I had seen ballet steps transposed – but lovingly and carefully transposed – into popular dance in such films as *Oklahoma* where Agnes de Mille brought something of the Ballet Russe to the Hollywood musical. *West Side Story* was to take forward the very American marriage of classical and popular dance – but although this might have been a subliminal bedding ground and although the glamorous photographs of dancers which ornamented the record sleeves presented some tantalising idea of what the real thing might be like, it was not until I saw a live production that I began to appreciate what riches there were. *Swan Lake* it was: smile if you like; it's wonderful!

I began to read but in a rather oblique way: which is to say I came across Nijinsky's notebook/diary and read on from there – into the heartland of the Diaghilev vortex. I was whirled into that imploding galaxy of talent – Benois, Fokine, Nijinsky, Picasso, Cocteau, Stravinsky. Ballet to me for the first year of full enthusiasm was as much to do with tracing the extraordinary combinations of talent which the Russian sorcerer threw into his alchemical pot as watching the dance. It was an enormous and unexpected bonus that having arrived at the sight and sound of a pleasure whose direct appeal, as anticipated, is to the senses, I should have discovered that some of the most flamboyant intellectual experiments in modern art found expression in the famous Russian Ballet troupe managed by Diaghilev. It was not only the riveting tortured words of Nijinsky whose line to adolescent sympathies was as direct as that of Van Gogh; not only the barbaric magic of Stravinsky and the wit of Cocteau – it was also the feeling of sophistication, of being in a metropolis of art, a gay and gamey metropolis, a place where ideas were turned into actions, where thoughts were staged and applauded or rejected, where the life of the mind confronted an audience through performance and everything gelled; it was all that a young provincial thought the world of 'art' ought to be – and who, when adolescent, is not provincial?

It would be untrue for me to claim that I have been in any way a 'balletomane'. Nevertheless that early interest, first kindled by the music and informed by reading about the adventures of Diaghilev and his Muscovyteers, clinched an ideal: the ideal vaguely imagined of what Real Ballet would be like. Since then, through television, chiefly, I have been able to pursue a pleasurable education.

Television's limitations as a transmitter of performance are so obvious that they need no stressing: the performers can look like rollicking Tom Thumbs, scenes designed for an harmonious interplay between chorus and principals have to be chopped up into close-ups or photographed from such a distance that all emotional contact is lost; the sound boxes on television sets are, generally, very poor; and one could go on if not ad infinitum at least to the point at which the question would have to be asked – what purpose is served?

The proof is in the AI. The AI is the audience Appreciation Index. Audiences are measured in bulk, and here ballet scores low – although, when you consider that programmes made about choreographers such as Richard Alston bring in an audience of between two and three million you have to take 'low' with a pinch of television salt. Yet by the standard of mainstream television, any audience under five million is a 'minority'. What the AI shows, however, is how much the programme was liked. It is not that ballet programmes score especially highly here – although they can – but they do clearly affect, enthuse and embrace people whose previous image of ballet was that of the artificial prancing before the privileged. Television's great gift is that it can make a subject domestic. There are those who hate and despise television for this very gift. But it is undeniable. In the privacy of your own home you can see ballets and documentaries about ballet that you would never have ventured to see had you been asked or given the chance to cross the threshold. The AI shows that television brings ballet to the people, and the wide upsurge of interest in ballet shows that it is also helping to bring the people to ballet.

A further way in which television has enlarged my own knowledge and interest has been in the making of programmes about ballet. I am in the enviable and fortunate position of editing an Arts programme which addresses itself to ballet and wants to take it on the most serious and the most engaging level possible. This has meant that I have edited and worked through programmes on MacMillan's *Mayerling* (on which I suggested the need for a critic and was rewarded by meeting – or employing – Clement Crisp who introduced a new perspective and edge into television ballet documentaries), on Richard Alston and his thoughtful, scrupulous work, on Baryshnikov and the American Ballet Theatre, on Robert Cohan and London Contemporary Dance, on Ninette de Valois, on Agnes de Mille, on Merce Cunningham – and across the board I have been ever more surely impressed by the riches to be found in ballet in this last quarter of the twentieth century. Traditions are lovingly perpetrated, departures carefully made, work is done with physical and intellectual intensity, innovations boldly attempted – and there is a great bonus to it all, a hum of enjoyment in the ballet/dance world whether it is in New York, London or Moscow. Young choreographers in Covent Garden, young dancers from the American mid-west, brilliant Russians straying across the border or staying to attempt to extend their own borders, are all attacking a world which demands ferocious physical application and ability, a talent to disguise strain and turn it into beautiful movement and ideas which have to work on and finally through the human body.

There is an optimistic revolution in the appreciation of ballet and this book, I believe, is both a guide and a tribute to that revolution.

Melvyn Bragg
23 March 1983

1

ENJOYING BALLET

Dancing is a manner of being.

Balzac

The only way to enjoy ballet is to go to the ballet. Whatever explanations and encouragement about ballet-going we may give in this book, nothing can convey to you the actual experience and excitement of sitting in a theatre and waiting for that magical moment when the houselights go dark, for the orchestra to start playing and the curtain to go up.

The trouble with people who have not gone to the ballet is that they seem to suspect that they have got to be 'clever', or have got to 'understand' or have even got to be part of a particular social class. This is absolute nonsense. If you want to go to the ballet then do so. Like all other forms of theatre, the ballet box office is open to everybody; there is no membership qualification to get in; there is no test paper to be answered when you leave. So why not try?

You can start anywhere. Several ballet and modern

dance companies in this country spend their whole year touring. If you live near a great metropolitan centre like London there is bound to be theatrical dance of one kind or another going on somewhere. If we can do anything in this book to help, it is to tell you something of the sort of thing you can expect to find, whether it be at the Royal Opera House, Covent Garden, London, or on the outermost edges of fringe experiment in studios or small arts centres.

People who go to the ballet take what they see for granted. They have come to appreciate one of the most basic means of expression of the human animal, because dancing is a response to many different situations and different feelings. The very origins of theatre are to be found in ancient forms of religious dance; the social dances of our Western civilisation are a natural expression of people's enjoyment in moving to music. Today, as always, dancing can be an integral part of people's lives and a direct manifestation of their emotions, from a knees-up in a pub to the dancing in the streets that can be seen on great occasions of national celebration: everyone danced in 1945 to celebrate the Allied victory in Europe on V.E. Night, and people danced with delight at parties to mark the wedding of the Prince of Wales in 1981.

Young people have always enjoyed especially exciting and energetic new dance styles, from the Charleston of the 1920s to the later crazes of Jitterbug, Rock 'n' Roll, and today's Disco dancing – just as our Victorian ancestors were caught up in Polkamania and, earlier, in very curious mediaeval dance manias.

It is very curious that no one is afraid of the word 'dance' and no one would object to the phrase 'let's go dancing'. But mention 'ballet' and hackles rise and prejudices, social and sexual, rear their heads. These prejudices spring from several misconceptions and from certain historic facts. Ballet, the Western theatrical dance form which developed over a period of four centuries, has always depended for its life upon State or Royal patronage and upon bourgeois metropolitan support in great opera houses in great cities. It has thus come to be seen as a cultural form remote from the experience of anyone outside a particular metropolitan area and even a particular class. Its language is the product of a

Patricia McBride and Helgi Tomasson of the New York City Ballet in the final *Rosenkavalier* section of George Balanchine's *Vienna Waltzes*.

refining process which has removed it entirely from the direct physical experience of ordinary mortals. To become a ballet dancer implies seven years of arduous training from an early age, whereas, given a certain amount of goodwill, anyone can dance at a social gathering. Furthermore, the physical image of both male and female dancers is so stylised, costuming so improbable in many cases, with its tights and slippers, tutus and pointe shoes, that it is not possible for the general public

Margot Fonteyn and Rudolf Nureyev in the Kingdom of Shades
scene from *La Bayadère*, created by Petipa in St Petersburg in 1877.
The scene is one of the great surviving masterpieces of classical
dance, and calls for meticulous dancing from the principals and the
supporting company of corps de ballet and soloists. The first

appearance of the 'shades' (ghosts) of the bayadères (temple
dancers) is celebrated as a *coup de théâtre*, as one by one 32 girls
descend a ramp, each first seen in arabesque, and the stage
gradually fills with mysterious white-clad figures, repeating these
arabesques in a swelling orchestration of movement.

to have that kind of identification with a ballet dancer which they can feel for actor, film star or athlete.

It is indeed strange that an art in which there are no words to misunderstand and which speaks directly to the eye, as does a football match or an Olympic gymnastic contest, still arouses some kind of apprehension. Too often people stay away from ballet because they think they will not 'understand' it, but they never seem to find this problem when watching ice dance championships, which are so popular on television, and neither are they afraid to express their opinions and disagree, sometimes, with the judges' decisions. If a new public would only start to look at dancing – any form of dancing – on the terms they bring to sport, enjoying its physical daring, appreciating the superb bodies working at maximum efficiency, there would be no further prejudices to overcome and we should not have the pleasure of writing this book.

It is better to look at dancing with a completely innocent eye than to puzzle and seek for meanings and thereby lose the prime delight in seeing beautiful bodies, beautifully trained, performing beautiful movement. Understanding will come with experience, but it is valueless unless the enjoyment is constant and increasing.

So what can you see in the ballet theatre? To paraphrase a comment about one famous daily newspaper – all human life is there. Ballets can set an audience rocking with laughter as they react to the sort of physical jokes that the great clowns of the cinema and television perform. You have but to watch a dancer looking suspiciously like Groucho Marx trying to stab his obstinately unstabbable wife to the accompaniment of Chopin piano music (in Jerome Robbins's *The Concert*), or watch a very small chap trying to manipulate the leggiest of ballerinas and getting into a terrible and slightly improper tangle in MacMillan's *Elite Syncopations*, while Scott Joplin rags are playing, to know what fun ballet can be.

But at the same performance you can have your blood run chill when you see the family in *My Brother, My Sisters*, also by MacMillan, as they play murderous children's games which become terrifyingly real. You can feel profound pity for Crown Prince Rudolf, heir to the Austro-Hungarian throne, in

Jerome Robbins subtitles his ballet *The Concert* 'The Perils of
Everybody'. Here, in the Royal Ballet's production, Vergie Derman is
the archetypal American matron about to receive what her
hen-pecked husband (Michael Coleman) hopes will be the *coup de
grâce*. This is one of the fantasies acted out by a group of people
attending a concert of Chopin piano music.

17

Above: Kenneth MacMillan's *Mayerling*, an epic work dealing with the tragic story of the heir to the Austro-Hungarian throne, Crown Prince Rudolf, was created for the Royal Ballet in 1978. At the wedding reception of Rudolf (David Wall, kneeling) and Princess Stephanie (Wendy Ellis, behind him), Rudolf flirts with his new wife's sister, Princess Louise (Genesia Rosato), while the Emperor Franz Josef (Michael Somes, right) stands aghast and Louise's husband (Derek Rencher, left) intervenes. Such complex relationships are part of the dramatic fabric of this exceptional narrative ballet.

Right: David Bintley, dancer and choreographer with the Sadler's Wells Royal Ballet, as the Widow Simone in Ashton's *La Fille mal gardée*. The widow is not a burlesque character but a lovable old duck who, despite her ambitions for her daughter to make a wealthy marriage, succumbs to the claims of true love at the end.

the full-length *Mayerling*, as you watch him brutalise his young bride and gradually decline into drug addiction and sexual obsession which lead to suicide.

Other types of love, such as the sunny good humour in Ashton's *La Fille mal gardée* or the gentle romance of his *The Two Pigeons*, are immediately recognisable to today's audience. You can also – and this is where ballet differs from every other delight in the theatre, cinema or television – be stimulated by the sheer verve and energy of male dancers or be enchanted by the grace of a ballerina in such favourites as *Swan Lake* or *Les Sylphides*. If you love music you will hear a

lot of the very best music in the theatre – and some of it very well played. If you like jazz or hard rock, or Mahler or Tchaikovsky or Stravinsky, or the most adventurous avant garde, ballet and contemporary dance companies will enable you to hear just such an extraordinary range of musical offerings and will, by a curious alchemy, help you to understand 'difficult' scores by seeing them interpreted in dance. It has been truly said of the work of the great Russian-American choreographer George Balanchine that his ballets are music made visible.

For the lover of painting and the graphic arts, ballet and dance companies represent an extraordinary touring exhibition. Many of the best-known artists of this century, from Picasso to Hockney and Andy Warhol, have provided designs for dance. One of the great visual experiences of this century was the revelation of colour which came with Léon Bakst's designs for *Schéhérazade* in 1910 when boring, fusty design was put to flight by his emotional mingling of greens and reds and purples. Anyone who goes to see the Merce Cunningham Dance Company will have a rare opportunity to understand the work of contemporary experimenters like Robert Rauschenberg and Jasper Johns, and part of the popularity of certain artists in this century was initially due to the exposure given to their work by ballet companies.

And because ballet deals with human bodies and their possibilities to express every kind of emotion, ballet must seem constantly fresh and constantly challenging to its audience. It is also constantly challenging to its practitioners, since dancing is a young person's game. By the age of forty, a dancer's technique is already on the wane because muscles lose their elasticity and the frame starts to rebel against the enormously taxing demands that have been made upon it since the early teens.

Once a boy or girl determines upon a dancing career and their determination has been supported by the opinions of teachers, who will know from the very first if a young person has any chance of a career in ballet, they have then committed themselves to a life of discipline as demanding and unrelenting as that of any champion athlete. They can never afford to relax their physical vigilance throughout their careers, and

Robert Kovich in Merce Cunningham's *Travelogue*. Robert Rauschenburg's designs often rely upon a chance assemblage of everyday objects.

every day of their professional life must begin with the hour and a half of sweated labour in class which prepares their bodies for the day's work. The male dancer is as tough and physically sturdy as any gymnast or footballer, and those people who want to make fun about the male ballet dancer have been misled by one of the secrets of his physical skill: the fact that he has learned at a considerable physical expense to *hide* any obvious effort. This applies not just to his own dancing but also to the many demands that are made upon him in partnering. Partnering, it must be remembered, involves not only dancing in harmony with the girl, or supporting her when she essays certain difficult feats, but also carrying her at arm's length above his head or catching her when she is moving at speed. Few athletes have the strength or daring to do this. It is strange to find in this century that, despite all these obvious proofs of strength and virility, the male dancer is still the victim of an odd kind of mistrust as well as of hoary music-hall jokes. This is a swing of history's pendulum, since initially the male dancer was the pre-eminent figure in the ballet theatre in the eighteenth century. Such dancers as Gaetano Vestris and Jean Dauberval were famed for bowling over every woman in sight. It is the nineteenth century and the Romantic movement, which raised the ballerina on to her toes and on to a pedestal as the personification of dance, which gradually degraded the male dancer so that he became eventually no more than a feeble and posturing denizen of a half world. The ultimate indignity came in the latter part of the nineteenth century when the role of the hero in certain ballets, especially in Paris, was taken by a pretty girl dressed *en travesti.*

It is from this period, which saw the emergence of the ballerina as the star performer in ballet, that the basic 'classical' repertory of the great ballet companies in the West is preserved. For this reason, perhaps, the central figure in ballet has come down to us as a female dancer. It is the efforts in this century of male dancers and choreographers that have set about reasserting a proper balance between male and female performers, and showing us that to be a male dancer is as exciting and creative a career for a man as to be an actor or a musician.

The classic repertory, that body of ballets which date from the nineteenth century and which have been preserved because of their dances and the challenge they offer dancers, as well as the beauty of their music – *The Sleeping Beauty* and *Coppélia,* for example – is one of the foundations of ballet going. The ballerinas who will dance the leading roles inevitably come and go; but the fascination of the ballets themselves remains and audiences return time after time to see and compare new interpretations. (The demands of ballets nowadays, however, require artists to identify themselves with characters far removed from the fairies and princes of the traditional repertory.)

The third act of *Coppélia* is a festival and divertissement culminating in a pas de deux for Swanilda and Franz. Peter Wright has staged a version for the Sadler's Wells Royal Ballet with designs by Peter Snow. This picture shows the corps de ballet at the beginning of the act.

We must here issue the warning that ballet is addictive. It was the English dance critic and enthusiast for ballet, Arnold Haskell (1903–80), who gave currency to the word 'balletomania' which is the terminal stage of the obsession, in his book of that title published in 1934. It is a work one can return to with constant pleasure and we recommend it to any reader. But even before that point is reached a ballet-goer who has once caught the bug knows that the more it is seen, the more ballet will be wanted. It is axiomatic that the dedicated ballet-goer will never miss a new interpretation of a great role or a new ballet. We found ourselves recently on the first sunny and radiant Saturday of the year giving up the beautiful afternoon in favour of yet another matinée of *Giselle,* a ballet which we have seen more than a hundred times, because a new dancer was making her début in the title role. We observed to each other, as we approached the entrance to the theatre, 'we must be mad', but we did not turn back – and did not regret the lost sunshine.

Ballet is increasingly popular as, indeed, are all forms of dance. The old belief that ballet was essentially London-based, and that touring was an activity which filled in the gaps between more important metropolitan seasons, has gone totally. Ballet companies today place great importance upon their journeys round the regions. Both London Festival Ballet and the Sadler's Wells Royal Ballet spend the greater part of the year away from their home base, and if there is anything which inhibits more extensive regional performance by large companies it is the decline in the number of suitable theatres rather than any unwillingness to travel on the part of ballet companies. In order to provide a large and popular theatre to show its wares the Royal Ballet has made good use of a circus tent, the Big Top. This has been used in Battersea Park in London, and in Plymouth, Newcastle upon Tyne, Cambridge and Edinburgh, to give seasons which otherwise would not have been possible. The conditions may not be absolutely ideal, but the stage is virtually the same size as that of the Royal Opera House and it is splendidly resilient, which dancers like. (A hard, unyielding stage brings immediate and dreadful injury; dancers need to feel the suggestion of a 'spring' under their feet.) The repertory and artists provided are of the best. One of the greatest performances of *Giselle* by the Royal Ballet in twenty years was in fact given in the Big Top, led by Natalia Makarova and Anthony Dowell.

An enormous contribution to the popularity of all forms of dance in the past decade has been the spread throughout the country of interest in and availability of contemporary dance. This has been the result of pioneering work by both the London Contemporary Dance Theatre and Ballet

Rambert, two troupes devoted to ballet's companion art, 'modern' or 'contemporary' dance. The relatively small size of these two companies enables them to play in theatres not suitable for the larger forces of a ballet company, but equally important has been the educational tradition which attaches to contemporary dance in the United States and which was implanted, with contemporary dance itself, in this country in the late 1960s.

The London Contemporary Dance Theatre was able in the 1970s to initiate a series of 'residencies' in which sections of the company were installed for a period of a week or more in colleges of education throughout the country. There they invited the public, local teachers and dance students to come and watch them at work during the routine rehearsals and creative sessions of the day; from there they went out to schools and colleges to teach and at the same time maintained a schedule of evening performances which would show the finished product of the day's labours. By thus taking dance to the people, they stimulated a tremendous public awareness of the pleasures of dance, and furthermore inspired many young people to view dance as a necessary part of their education and a possible and very attractive career. It is gratifying that much support was given to this aspect of dance activity by the regional arts associations whose task it is to foster the enjoyment and appreciation of all the arts in their area. Furthermore, there came a proliferation of dance activity resulting from the teachings of the London School of Contemporary Dance, which meant that small groups and solo artists were readily available to work throughout the country. Another stimulus to public interest came with the educational programmes, spearheaded by the sadly defunct Ballet for All, which toured extensively to show and explain dance. Latterly educational programmes have been offered by each of the major dance companies to schools and to specially interested groups.

Thus we have today a situation where dance can be found in the curriculum of comprehensive schools and in primary schools; it is a subject for study in colleges and Institutes of Further Education and can lead to a degree course. It has also won recognition as being worthy of proper notice by the media: every newspaper and journal which takes the arts seriously provides dance coverage and criticism.

However, it is television that must be thanked for the greatest expansion in the audience for dancing. Through such admirable enterprises as the BBC's biennial *Dance Month* (which can show up to thirty dance programmes in a month, ranging from the avant-garde to *The Red Shoes*), and the transmissions of the South Bank Show from London Weekend Television (which won one of its several Prix Italia awards for a two-hour programme about MacMillan's *Mayerling,* directed by Derek Bailey), millions of viewers have watched ballet, from major presentations of the great classics like *Swan Lake* and *The Sleeping Beauty* to documentaries which have sought to widen public interest and understanding by exploring something of the world of ballet and the dancer.

It is important to mention the inestimable debt owed to the star performer. Throughout ballet's history certain artists have attracted the intensest public adoration, from those Russian balletomanes who acquired one of the shoes worn by Marie Taglioni, darling of the 1830s, had it cooked in a sauce and then solemnly ate it, to fans who surrendered precious ration coupons to dancers during the Second World War, and to the adoring hordes who swarm around such stars today as Nureyev, Baryshnikov, Makarova and Dowell. It is these artists who are vital in the commercial considerations for ballet; their name on a programme means a full house. But while television may bring these great artists to a vaster audience than they can ever reach in their theatrical career, and their appearances on the screen can stimulate a new public, nothing can ever replace that vivid experience of sitting in a theatre and waiting for the curtain to go up on a ballet. There is an implicit give and take between ballet and its television

Right: Mikhail Baryshnikov airborne in the third act of *Swan Lake.* Baryshnikov, born in Riga in 1948, trained at the Kirov School in Leningrad. He has conquered audiences all over the world through his phenomenal technique and exceptional artistry. He became director of American Ballet Theatre in 1980.

Anthony Dowell as the boy in Jerome Robbins's *Afternoon of a Faun*.
In 1953, Jerome Robbins took the Debussy music, which had been
the basis for Nijinsky's ballet *L'Après-midi d'un faune*, 1912, and
made an entirely fresh ballet about the meeting between two very
young dancers in a ballet studio. The treatment was contemporary,
but traces of the Nijinsky theme can be found in the mood of this
luminous new version.

audience so that anyone sufficiently stimulated by the television showing *must* make the effort to go to a theatre to see
live ballet. And although ballet is a luxury item, it need not be
prohibitively expensive. There are many schemes throughout
Britain, and throughout the Western world, which will allow
individuals or groups to obtain concessionary rates to go to the
ballet – and it is worth inquiring from any company for details
of these schemes. The vital thing is to *go,* and the purpose of
this book is to encourage a new audience. Ballet needs new
blood in the auditorium as on stage. There is nothing more
depressing than an ultra-conservative audience which refuses
to look at anything new and adventurous – it knows what it
likes and it likes what it knows. If we can help dispel the mis-
givings of a newcomer to the ballet then we – and the newcomer – have done something to expand ballet's horizons. The
great fear for the newcomer is having to 'understand' ballet in
order to enjoy it. The reverse is true: enjoyment comes first.
And ballet can be very enjoyable.

2

THE MAJOR BALLET COMPANIES

Dancing serves no necessary use, no profitable, laudable, or pious end at all; it issues only from the inbred pravity, vanity, wantonness, incontinency, pride, profaneness or madness of men's depraved natures.

William Prynne, *Histriomastix* of 1633

Ballet is by tradition an art of the opera house. Historically, ballet and opera grew up side by side in the chief theatres of Europe, but there has ever been a Montague and Capulet relationship, with fighting for stage time and revenue, and even for kudos. So it is odd to note that despite this disagreement these two halves of the lyric theatre have never been divorced: the nearest to a separation may be the building in the 1960s of the State Theater at Lincoln Center, New York, primarily for the New York City Ballet. The theatre was designed by the distinguished American architect Philip Johnson, in consultation with George Balanchine, great choreographer and guiding creative force behind NYCB, as a house for ballet more than opera, albeit the New York City

Opera also gives its seasons there. Elsewhere, opera and ballet share the same theatre and the same facilities in an alternation of ballet and opera evenings.

This is the case at the Royal Opera House, Covent Garden; the Paris Opéra; the Leningrad State Kirov Theatre; the Bolshoy Theatre in Moscow; and the Royal Theatre in Copenhagen. These theatres are the homes of Europe's greatest ballet companies, but almost every opera house has a ballet company of some kind or another. This is true of the Royal Theatre in Stockholm, which has a fine ballet company, as it is of La Scala, Milan, where the ballet takes a very secondary place to opera. It is true in Stuttgart, where the ballet is more famous than the opera, as in those many other German houses where opera is the dominant partner.

Sadly, Britain's history of opera and ballet in its regions is lamentable, whereas every major city in France, Germany and Italy can boast an opera house and a resident company. Belgium, for example, has no fewer than three national companies, the Royal Ballets of Wallonie and Flanders and the Ballet du XXe Siècle, which is based on the

Artists of the Ballet du XXe Siècle in Maurice Béjart's *The Triumphs of Petrach*. This picture gives a good idea of the spectacular size of a typical Béjart work.

Théâtre Royal de la Monnaie in Brussels. This last offers a particularly interesting insight into the audience and the housing of ballet. Under the leadership of Maurice Béjart, the Ballet du XXe Siècle has performed amid the plush and lustres of Brussels' opera house, but also has gone out into a circus to appeal to a larger and younger audience who might be repelled by the supposed stuffiness of an opera house, and has subsequently played in arenas and sports stadia throughout the world.

Nevertheless, the traditional classic academic ballet is an opera house art because it needs opera house facilities, opera house size and opera house security – a security owed to State subvention, regular audiences, and location in a great capital city. Thus the Royal Ballet at Covent Garden, though it makes prestigious tours abroad, is best seen in its home theatre. Its productions are scaled to the size of the Royal Opera House, its artists feel at home on the stage and there is a tradition of performance (and of attendance at the ballet) which is integral to the company's identity. By comparison with the Paris Opéra, the State Theater, and the Kirov and Bolshoy Theatres, Covent Garden is a medium-size theatre with a very medium-size stage, and its financial resources are medium-size compared with the vast sums made available in Paris, Russia, Austria and Germany to support the lyric theatre as a cause for national pride.

For anyone who thinks that 'ballet' is some kind of formula, an art of hard and fast rules and absolutely unchanging identity, the chance to see any of the great national companies will show how false this view is. Even the way in which each ensemble presents what we may think of as an established work of art, like *Giselle* or *Swan Lake,* is markedly different. Schooling, national temperament and the company's view of the dramatic content of a ballet will all contribute to the extreme differences of performance. *Swan Lake,* that most popular of ballets, is performed all over the world and no two productions are really alike. There may be an accepted basic text for part of the ballet – only the second act with its great *pas de deux* between the Swan Princess Odette and Prince Siegfried is universally respected – but styles of dancing and styles of production vary enormously and there is also an added hazard in that companies often seek to 'update' the ballet. The result is productions as widely and amazingly different as those of the New York City Ballet, which gives a single-act view of the lakeside scene with interpolated music from the fourth act of the score and much choreography by Balanchine; Peter Darrell's view, for Scottish Ballet, of the Prince as a drug addict who dreams much of the action; John Neumeier's Freudian interpretation with the Hamburg Ballet which equates the Prince with Ludwig of Bavaria; the Leningrad Kirov Ballet's traditional view which contrasts with the Moscow Bolshoy Ballet's more psychologically oriented version by Grigorovich; the Canadian National Ballet's production by the Danish dancer, Erik Bruhn, in which the Prince's mother becomes the villain; and the Royal Ballet's production which combines much of the traditional text with additional choreography by Ashton and de Valois.

And different as these productions are, no less different is the manner of dancing them. The double role of Odette-Odile is one of the supreme challenges of the ballerina's art. It should only be danced by the very grandest artists, and they can bring enormous variety of interpretation and dance manner. The first great English Odette-Odile was Alicia Markova, a dancer of exquisite style. Very different was her successor, Margot Fonteyn, who stressed the importance of Odette's tragedy. In Russia, Maya Plisetskaya of the Bolshoy gave an interpretation of tremendous physical intensity, while in Leningrad Irina Kolpakova epitomised the aristocracy and nobility of the style of the company for which the ballet was originally created.

The other great ingredient of *Swan Lake* is the corps de ballet in the lakeside scenes and it is this, quite as much as the eminence of the ballerina, which shows a company fitted to perform this ballet. Impeccable schooling and unity in dance manner are essential. By their corps de ballet, ye shall know them. Any company can be fortunate enough to acquire a great ballerina; it takes years of hard work, dedicated teaching and integrity of purpose to produce a great corps de ballet. It is the participation of the corps in such works as the second act of *Giselle*, *Swan Lake* and the Kingdom of Shades scene from *La Bayadère* which are touchstones of a company's

This photograph was taken at Covent Garden in 1956 when the Bolshoy Ballet gave its first season in the West. It shows the corps de ballet of Wilis in the second act of *Giselle*.

importance, and which make the ensembles of the Kirov and Bolshoy, New York City Ballet and the Royal Ballet truly great.

A ballet company depends upon three things. A home theatre, a school, and a resident choreographer. Each of these represents a different but essential stability. The home means that the company is not rootless, however much it may tour, and its productions are geared and gauged essentially to a certain size. It is rather like knowing the size of a room and understanding the proportions of the furniture you can put into it. The school provides the lifeblood of the company by training young dancers (ideally from the age of eleven) who will be used to feed the company's ranks with dancers whose bodies speak the same physical 'language' as the rest of the troupe. The choreographer is essential to produce the new works which are the artistic and imaginative future of the ballet. He reflects the creative attitudes of the company but he also must seek to extend them.

the Royal Ballet

Britain's Royal Ballet, as you will see more fully in Chapter 4, grew up in Rosebery Avenue, London, at Sadler's Wells Theatre. It was the opportunity which came in 1946 to re-open the Royal Opera House, Covent Garden, after the war as a national lyric theatre which brought it to its present home and its present international importance. In its fifty-year existence the Royal Ballet has emerged as one of the most exceptional artistic achievements of the century. It is based firmly upon the traditional attitudes of the nineteenth-century ballet and it preserves several of the famous masterpieces of that period as part of its wide-ranging repertory. It also presents certain major works created over the years by the greatest international choreographers of this century, but its vitality essentially resides in the native choreographers whose works it has commissioned and encouraged.

The Royal Ballet was fortunate in its early days in that it had Ninette de Valois to develop the dramatic gifts of English dancers (in works like *The Rake's Progress*) and also has had Frederick Ashton to develop the English lyric style in such short ballets as *Les Rendezvous, Symphonic Variations* and *A Month in the Country*. Ashton also produced the vital development of full-length ballets inspired by the nineteenth-century example, and his *Cinderella, La Fille mal gardée* and *The Two Pigeons* are enduring favourites. It is to Kenneth MacMillan, the Royal Ballet's other major choreographer, that we look for a further development of the company's style in expressive and dramatic power. He has enhanced the possibilities of three-act ballet in *Anastasia, Manon, Mayerling* and

**the
Royal
Ballet**

Isadora. In his short works he has also shown how the emotions and the sexual drive of his characters can be revealed in dance.

Sustaining this range of repertory and also reflecting it is the actual dance style of the company. A Royal Ballet trained dancer can be recognised by a kind of academic correctness that is never extreme and is always informed by a musicality and a clarity of line; these are the outward signs of the essential restraint and conservatism of the English school. English dancers excel in lyric roles but they are also exceptional dramatic artists when called upon to be so in such works as those cited above by de Valois, Ashton and MacMillan.

The Royal Ballet is closely linked in people's minds

A 'Prom' audience at the Royal Opera House, Covent Garden.

with the Royal Opera House. Although the company has
toured worldwide, it has to maintain its presence in London as
the greatest ballet company in Britain. But even though seat
prices at Covent Garden can be very expensive, it is possible
to see the Royal Ballet at the Royal Opera House reasonably.
The upper part of the house is very fairly priced, and sight-
lines from the very top centre of the house (the back row of the
Amphitheatre) are good. Moreover, for popular performances,
standing room is available, once the house is sold out, at the
back of the Stalls Circle. Each year the generosity of the
Midland Bank has sponsored a run of 'Promenade' performances when all the stalls seats are removed and ballet and
opera lovers can stand, kneel, squat or recline as the fancy
and the space take them and, for the princely sum of £1.00 (as
we go to press), can see some of the current repertory of both
the Royal Ballet and the Royal Opera. Furthermore, membership of the Friends of Covent Garden organisation (details of
which can be obtained from their office at the Royal Opera
House) brings facilities to see rehearsals and also provides
special booking rates for students.

**the
Royal
Ballet**

Sadler's Wells Royal Ballet

The essential 'other half' of the Royal Ballet's identity is the
smaller Sadler's Wells Royal Ballet which tours for the greater
part of the year through the regions and abroad.

In 1946 when the then Sadler's Wells Ballet transferred to the Royal Opera House, Covent Garden, Ninette de
Valois could not leave her ancestral theatre empty of ballet
and she initiated a second company to take up residence
there. It was younger in personnel and served as a nursery for
talent, providing opportunities for young dancers and young
choreographers who were later to contribute much to the
Covent Garden company – we need only cite the ballerinas
Nadia Nerina and Svetlana Beriosova, and the choreographers John Cranko and Kenneth MacMillan to indicate the
importance of the company's work. Since those early days,
despite inevitable changes, the 'second company' has always
been a vital force within the Royal Ballet organisation and

**Sadler's Wells
Royal Ballet**

today the company, based again on Sadler's Wells as its home, fulfils an important function in nurturing both dancers and choreographers and in making Royal Ballet standards of performance and production available throughout the country where there are theatres able to sustain weekly or two-weekly seasons by the troupe.

Both sections of the Royal Ballet provide not only the classic traditional repertory which is so vital to the company's image, but also representative works from the major choreographers of the twentieth century (Fokine's *Les Sylphides* for example) and major works by choreographers who have given the Royal Ballet its British identity, from Ninette de Valois and Frederick Ashton to Kenneth MacMillan. In the case of the Sadler's Wells Royal Ballet, there are works by the new generation of Royal choreographers led by David Bintley and Michael Corder.

It is not too far-fetched to say that the audiences around the country who see the work of the Sadler's Wells Royal Ballet have a very good view of the future of the company and of its potential, since it is with this section of our national ballet that the apprentice works of interesting new talent are to be seen. Naturally enough, the forces of the Royal Ballet at Covent Garden and the stage resources there are needed for the largest and most lavish developments in the repertory.

the Royal Ballet School

The firm basis of a school was the prerequisite which Ninette de Valois sought when she set about building a national ballet. She opened her own school in London in 1926, and when she was able to move into Sadler's Wells Theatre five years later she moved that school into the theatre as the bedrock for her achievement. As the company grew the school developed and fulfilled its prime function of feeding the emergent young company with young dancers. The company's style evolved through the ballets of de Valois and Frederick Ashton and the nineteenth-century classics, and this was in turn reflected back into the school, especially when former members of the company returned to teach there at the end of their dancing careers.

Today the school comprises two establishments. The junior school, housed at White Lodge (a former Royal residence) in Richmond Park, offers complete education and ballet training for boys and girls from the age of eleven; the upper school in West London is non-residential and admits not only the sixteen-year-olds from White Lodge but a considerable intake of apprentice dancers of the same age from the rest of the country and elsewhere. (Any child who passes the very stringent audition for White Lodge will automatically receive the grants necessary to support it at that school.)

The Royal Ballet School is the only establishment in this country which is totally linked to its parent ballet troupe in the traditional fashion, which obtains also with the other great world companies.

London Festival Ballet

London Festival Ballet was formed in 1950 from the nucleus of dancers who had been recruited to support a tour by Alicia Markova and Anton Dolin – legendary names in the world of ballet. By 1950 a company had been started (it owes its name to Markova's inspired realisation that with the impending Festival of Britain in 1951 'Festival' would be a magic word) which was to endear itself to an immense public throughout the world. The company knew that – without any subvention – it must rely upon star names and proven ballets to justify it at the box office, and in the next years Markova and Dolin were joined by some of the greatest international names in the world of ballet, seen in their most celebrated traditional roles.

Over the next thirty years the Festival Ballet became associated with popular seasons at the Royal Festival Hall on London's South Bank and latterly with seasons at the London Coliseum. The company laboured for many years without any subsidy, but eventually the Greater London Council, and then the Arts Council, acknowledged the undoubted merits and appeal of Festival Ballet and provided help. The company repertory has always recognised the fact that there exists a large middle-brow public, and has responded to this public with a middle of the road repertory. It was Festival Ballet which proved the continued efficacy of the ballets created by Mikhail Fokine for the Diaghilev Ballet Russe (see Chapter 4) and in recent years has staged very impressive productions of *Giselle* and *La Sylphide*, two masterpieces of the Romantic era. The company has also staged *The Sleeping Beauty* and *Romeo and Juliet* in versions by Rudolf Nureyev, and has joined that super-star in seasons around the world.

London Festival Ballet is a hard-working company, dancing every night and touring extensively, and its enthusiasm in performance and its evident affection for its public brings the response of full houses and enduring popular success. It does not have a school and relies on recruiting its dancers from various British vocational schools as well as from Common Market countries. It continues to maintain a regular and valuable relationship with the Royal Festival Hall and the Coliseum for its London seasons, and it has established an excellent educational programme whereby dancers and lecturers travel to schools, community centres, colleges and institutes to give insights into the world of ballet itself.

Ballet Rambert

The oldest ballet company in Britain – it dates from 1926 – the Ballet Rambert was the creation of Marie Rambert. Through the remarkable gifts of her early students, she sought to apply the standards which she had absorbed from her seasons with the Diaghilev Ballet Russe in 1912–13 to ballet in London.

During the late 1920s Rambert inspired creativity and imposed artistic integrity on the first flowerings of British ballet. It was she who launched such choreographic talents as Frederick Ashton, Antony Tudor, Walter Gore and Andrée Howard – all contributors to the very first achievements of ballet in London – and supervised the production of occasional performances of exceptional merit which featured the finest dancers in the country at that time. On the pocket handkerchief stage of the Mercury Theatre at Notting Hill Gate in

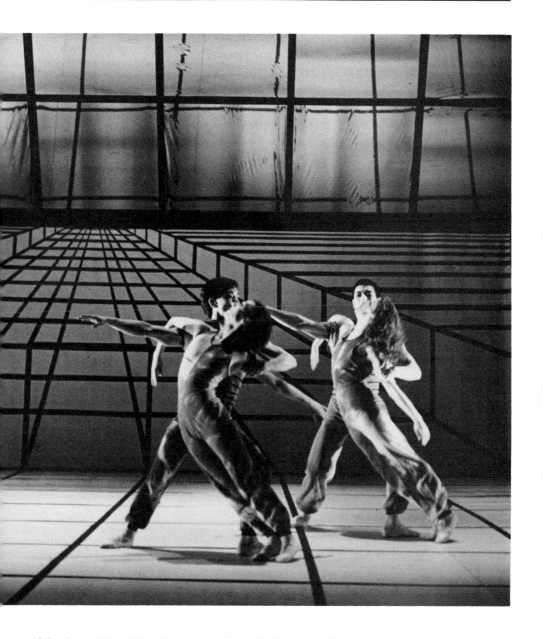

Members of the Ballet Rambert in Richard Alston's *Bell High*, set to
two works for clarinet by Peter Maxwell Davies. This is a good
example of the clear and well-patterned dances which characterise
the work of Alston, a graduate of the London School of
Contemporary Dance who has become resident choreographer of the
Ballet Rambert.

West London owned by her husband, the author Ashley
Dukes, which measured only eighteen feet square, she presented to an élite audience significant ballets, some of which –
Tudor's *Jardin aux Lilas* and *Dark Elegies* – survive to this
day.

From these intimate beginnings there emerged a
small company which perpetuated an idea of vivid creativity
which lasted, despite many vicissitudes, into the 1960s.

Under the directorship of Norman Morrice, another
Rambert choreographic discovery, Ballet Rambert then
shaped a new image which it has maintained to this day,
drawing increasingly upon the manner of contemporary
dance.

Ballet Rambert today remains modest in size and is
therefore able to visit comparatively small theatres as well as
major regional houses. It maintains regular annual seasons at
Sadler's Wells Theatre, and continues that pursuit of new
choreography which was characteristic of its very first seasons
half a century ago, through a remarkable number of workshop
and experimental performances. Its repertory since 1966 has
encompassed the creations of Glen Tetley, an American
choreographer who did much to break down the barriers
which formerly existed between classical and 'modern' dance
techniques, and a variety of British choreographers such as
Norman Morrice, Christopher Bruce and Richard Alston. In
1981 the dancer and choreographer Robert North, best known
for his work with London Contemporary Dance Theatre,
assumed direction of the company.

regional companies

The expression 'dance explosion' was widely and unwisely
used to describe the increase in public interest in dance in the
1960s and 1970s. In fact dance, like every other art, is subject
to the whims of public taste as can be deduced from the pendulum swings of taste between ballet and opera in the
nineteenth century. The work of touring ballet companies and
educational programmes did much to whet a public appetite
and the wish to cater more seriously for a regional public led

to the establishing of ballet companies away from London.

One such, Western Theatre Ballet, grew up in Bristol in the 1960s with a highly theatrical repertory and its eventual success owed everything to the vision of its founder, the late Elizabeth West and her choreographer Peter Darrell. Elizabeth West (1927–62) preached regional ballet long before any Government or local agencies saw the wisdom of her views. Eventually in 1969, Western Theatre Ballet was officially transferred to Glasgow and became Scottish Ballet, whose work thereafter has been a successful blend of traditionalism and experiment for very differing audiences in Scotland and throughout the world. Peter Darrell, who succeeded Elizabeth West as director of Western Theatre Ballet, remains Scottish Ballet's director and principal choreographer.

Another development from the example of Western Theatre Ballet was the setting up in 1969 of what is now Northern Ballet Theatre based in Manchester. The company was initiated by Laverne Meyer, a former dancer and choreographer with Western Theatre Ballet, as the first regionally based ballet company in Britain. Its subsequent career showed a move away from a theatrical and contemporary image to its present identity as a classical troupe offering popular fare.

national companies

In the middle years of this century, when international touring by ballet companies was still financially viable, all great companies came to London and some made regional trips as well. This, alas, is no longer feasible unless sustained by massive sponsorship. Hence there is a danger of the ballet public becoming insular in taste, although television does valuable work in bringing the dance of many nations to our screens. The really dedicated ballet-goer makes many sacrifices in order to go to New York, Copenhagen, Paris or Russia to see companies of vast importance who appear far too rarely in London, for these companies are the great examples of the different national styles of ballet.

national companies

A ballet company lives or dies through its school and its choreographers. Both of these are absolutely essential. Fine schooling in a traditional repertory can bring its own rewards, as in Copenhagen and in Leningrad; great choreography as a continuing creative tradition is needed to give a company an artistic identity for the present and the future. This is the fortunate position of the Royal Ballet and the New York City Ballet, both of which are sustained by a creative strength. Naturally enough, the school is the bedrock upon which any company must exist. It was the establishment of schools by royal edict in the seventeenth and eighteenth centuries which made possible the schools for the ballet companies in France, Russia, Denmark and Sweden, and thus produced the material for their national companies. Similarly, it was the determination of Lincoln Kirstein and George Balanchine in America and Ninette de Valois in Britain to establish schools which prepared the first steps of two great national companies, the New York City Ballet and the Royal Ballet.

Paris Opéra, France

The oldest of ballet schools is that associated with the Paris Opéra, which effectively dates from 1713 when a school was created to provide professional dancers for the opera-ballets of the period. It has been influenced across the years by such outside forces as the virtuoso Italian dance manner, and today the school of the Paris Opéra continues to produce dancers of exceptional technical prowess. But though the training at the Paris Opéra school is superb and the dancers who enter the company make up a very fine ensemble, it must be said that the Opéra company lacks a certain artistic definition. It was dominated and directed for more than a quarter century (1930–58) by the Russian-born Serge Lifar, Diaghilev's last brilliant protégé who, as dancer and choreographer, rescued the Opéra ballet from stagnation and made it a positive and admirable force in French cultural life. Magnificent dancers, fine design, the collaboration of leading French artists, Lifar's own heroic neo-classic dance manner and his stellar presence were contributory factors to the achievements of the Opéra ballet until the end of the 1950s. Thereafter an indecisive artistic policy has seen the Opéra accepting choreography from many different sources – from the American modern dancers Merce Cunningham and Douglas Dunn to the Bolshoy ballet's Yury Grigorovich and the Royal Ballet's Kenneth MacMillan. Standards of dancing continue very high – the Opéra manner is polished, elegant – but there is a lack of that creative assurance which only a native choreographer can bring to a company.

Russia

Leningrad (St Petersburg until 1914, Petrograd until 1924) was the centre of ballet in Russia as the old Imperial capital. In 1738 a school was instituted under a French dancing-master to educate children of palace servants and from this evolved a company whose magnificence owes much to the Russians' willingness to accept French dancing-masters and choreographers in the nineteenth century. St Petersburg preserved the honour of ballet when it was declining elsewhere in the West by the end of the nineteenth century, and the preservation

The Vaganova School in Leningrad is a direct continuation of the Imperial Ballet School. The school is named after Agrippina Vaganova, a former ballerina, and a teacher whose methods are the basis of ballet teaching throughout Russia.

Russia   of this great nineteenth-century inheritance is particularly important when considering the Leningrad company today.

The Revolution of 1917 brought changes but none so radical as to obliterate the aristocratic traditions of the Petersburg style. Leningrad's dancers today, sublimely trained, remain the exemplars of the academic dance.

Moscow, in Tsarist times a poor second to St Petersburg, has blossomed as a home for ballet with the transfer there of the Soviet Government and the importation to its ballet company of dancers, teachers and choreographers from Leningrad. Moscow style was historically always different from that of St Petersburg; that difference still remains. Essentially the Moscow style is more exultant, more Dionysiac; its huge school and its huge company are geared to fill not only the vastness of the Bolshoy stage but the even greater expanse of the Moscow Palace of Congresses, which seats 6,000 and offers an immense stage for dance – hence the space-devouring energies of the Moscow dancers at their best. (At their worst, they can look athletically vulgar to Western eyes.)

In Russia the repertories of the Leningrad Kirov Ballet and the Moscow Bolshoy often contain the same ballets but they are rather different in presentation. The Leningrad dancers still excel in the performance of the nineteenth-century classics, bringing to them a refinement and a distilled, aristocratic manner very distinct from the more extreme and emotional approach of the Bolshoy. It is like the difference between brilliant moonlight and the blaze of the sun. The Kirov also has a modern repertory of considerable range and Leningrad has often provided the choreographic talent which has then been transferred to Moscow. Today the Kirov has as its artistic director Oleg Vinogradov, who has produced interesting new choreographies, first at the smaller Maly (Mikhailovsky) Theatre in Leningrad where he created adventurous stagings of *Romeo and Juliet* and Britten's *Prince of the Pagodas,* and subsequently at the Kirov itself.

Two other Leningraders have been vital in forming the present Bolshoy repertory: Leonid Lavrovsky, creator of a famous *Romeo and Juliet,* and Yury Grigorovich, who is currently artistic director of the company. It is Grigorovich who

Alla Sizova and Yuri Solovyov of the Kirov Ballet in a still from the Russian film of *The Sleeping Beauty*.

has produced the ideological blockbusters, *Spartacus* and *Ivan the Terrible,* and the abstract *Romeo and Juliet,* which are today so central to the Bolshoy's identity. The roaring lines of rebellious slaves in *Spartacus* and the Moscow townsfolk in *Ivan the Terrible* are given with a passionate conviction by every dancer; they transform predictable choreography. The Moscow dancers surge across the stage, men and women buoyed up on tremendous jumps; it is an exultant, physically exhilarating and affirmative style.

Russia

Denmark

Very different is the company in Copenhagen. The Royal Danish Ballet traces its origins back to the eighteenth century but its vital formative influence remains August Bournonville (see pp. 84–85) who, between 1830 and 1877, created both a repertory and a style of dancing which survives beautifully to this day. It is a most significant comment upon this 'school' that, despite the comparative smallness of the Danish Ballet, it consistently produces dancers of the first quality – especially the men, who are the admiration of the world. Bournonville's training is particularly rewarding for men, since it develops exceptional strength, speed, intricate footwork, *élévation* and *ballon* – these last two terms signifying the dancers' ability to jump and their bounding elasticity of movement.

For women, the style is extremely charming and graceful and its tendency towards cosiness was dissipated during the twenty years in which the great Russian teacher, Vera Volkova, worked in Copenhagen.

The other distinctive quality of the Royal Danish dancers is their dramatic skill, whether in tragedy or in comedy. Every least role in the Bournonville repertory is played with loving care and treasured by its interpreters. In such masterpieces as *Napoli* or *A Folk Tale* or *Kermesse in Bruges* or *La*

Left: Boris Akimov as Crassus in Grigorovitch's *Spartacus,* as staged by the Bolshoy Ballet. The power of the Moscow style is well used in the big leaps which suggest Crassus's brutal and evil nature.

Niels Kehlet and Solveig Ostergaard of the Royal Danish Ballet airborne in the duet from Bournonville's *Flower Festival in Genzano*. The lightness and ebullience of their jump reflects an essential quality of the Bournonville style.

Sylphide we see the beautiful combination of an exhilarating dance style and this no less exhilarating dramatic manner. The Royal Danish Ballet has inevitably been dominated by its Bournonville traditions but it consistently makes attempts to extend its repertory. Both Harald Lander (choreographer and director between 1931–52) and his protégé and later successor Flemming Flindt (director/choreographer from 1965–78), sought to give the company new Danish ballets – although few have survived. A parallel influence upon the repertory

has been the invitation to distinguished foreign choreogra-
phers to create for the company: Ashton made his *Romeo and
Juliet* as early as 1955; Balanchine maintained a consistent
interest in the company for fifty years; and more recently
Jerome Robbins, Roland Petit, Kenneth MacMillan and John
Neumeier have all contributed to the repertory. One reason
why choreographers are so happy to work with the Royal
Danes is that they know that once in the Danish repertoire
their ballets will be maintained and properly cared for – David
Lichine's charming *Graduation Ball,* so grossly over-played
elsewhere, retains in Copenhagen its essential youth and
freshness.

the New York City Ballet

At nearly the same time that Ninette de Valois was setting out
to establish a British classical dance company and school, a
parallel activity was happening in the United States of America. Lincoln Kirstein, a man of the arts whose love of ballet had
made him determined that the classic academic style should
be implanted in American soil, invited George Balanchine to
come to America to establish a school from which would
develop a company. Balanchine was a product of the greatest
traditions in ballet, as a result of his training in St Petersburg:
he entered the Imperial School in 1914, graduated from it into
the post-Revolutionary Soviet State Ballet, and came to the
West in 1923 where he swiftly became the ballet-master for
the last six years of the Diaghilev Ballet Russe. Kirstein saw
that here was the ideal man, in 1933, to bring the grandest
manner of the academic dance to the new soil of the USA. A
school and company emerged which are today the School of
American Ballet and the New York City Ballet, enterprises
dominated by Balanchine's genius as a choreographer and his
belief in ballet as, essentially, a plotless response of dancing
bodies to music. Though this manner may sound austere, it is
not so. The extreme variety of Balanchine's choreographies –
which happily range from the succinct *Agon,* by Stravinsky, to
the popular tunes and exuberance of *Stars and Stripes* and

Above: Suzanne Farrell and Peter Martins of the New York City Ballet in *Agon*, choreographed by Balanchine to music by Stravinsky.

Right: Darci Kistler and Sean Lavery in Peter Martins' *Symphony No. 1*, which formed a part of the New York City Ballet's Tchaikovsky Festival in 1981.

**the
New York
City
Ballet**

Union Jack – is displayed by dancers magnificently prepared in the School of American Ballet. The training reflects Balanchine's concern for strength, speed and brilliance of execution, and to this end the school has drawn pedagogues from Russia and Denmark as well as many former members of the company.

development of ballet companies worldwide

These eminent companies and schools reflect a worldwide pattern in the field of classical ballet. In Canada and Australia there are national ballets and national schools which have emulated the Royal Ballet's example. The influence of the Moscow and Leningrad troupes is apparent not only throughout the USSR, where every Republic has a dance troupe or a ballet company, but also in those other countries behind the Iron Curtain where Soviet ideology encouraged the expansion of ballet companies in the years after 1945. The importance of Soviet teaching methods – all sprung from the precepts of Agrippina Vaganova (see p. 129) – was very apparent.

Parallel with the development of national companies since the death of Diaghilev in 1929 (see Chapter 4) has been the continuing pattern of independent companies who have toured widely, their existence often owing much to private fortunes and patronage, although dogged by the growing financial strain of touring ballet.

Today the most successful and popular of these companies is American Ballet Theatre, founded in 1939 and for forty years sustained by Lucia Chase, its director until 1980. Other American troupes like the Joffrey Ballet and those

Right: Danish-trained Peter Martins and Suzanne Farrell, two of the New York City Ballet's most exceptional principals, in Balanchine's *Chaconne*, set to music from Gluck's *Orpheus and Eurydice*.

development
of ballet
companies
worldwide

based in major cities outside New York help satisfy a con-stantly growing demand for ballet throughout the United States.

In Europe one company tours extensively: an ensemble dedicated to the choreographic utterances of one man, Maurice Béjart, whose ballets and whose tremendous appeal to a young audience has brought the company – the Ballet du XXe Siècle – to international fame. The troupe is devoted – in every sense – to Béjart, though he is no longer its director (he retired from this post after twenty years, handing over to the company's male star, Jorge Donn, though he remains the choreographic guru to the troupe).

Béjart's ballets can seem, to certain critical observers, banal, the philosophising behind them confused. Yet the dedication of the dancers, and the undoubted appeal of the company to a youthful audience uninterested in the staid classic fodder seen in opera houses, has made Béjart and his company a force to be reckoned with in the world of Western ballet. His dancers are drawn from Europe and America; they are welded into an ensemble by their involvement in the company's very strong ethos – earnest, marvellously well-intentioned about love, life and art. The male contingent is particularly strong and to be admired in the otherwise wilful and exasperating revisions of established themes torn from major works of art, or from re-workings of the accepted ballet classics. *Nijinsky, Clown of God; Trionfi; Petrushka; Firebird; Bolero; Our Faust;* and many more assaults on popular myths or famous figures, are witness to the popular success of the Béjart method. However, it must be said that many European (and especially French) critics are thrilled and excited by every Béjart work, while the Soviet book *Divertissement* by Vadim Gayevsky (1981) highlights a grave dissatisfaction with the Grigorovich repertory in Moscow and mentions only two choreographers of our time who are thought worthy advo-cates of the 'new' in ballet – George Balanchine and Maurice Béjart.

Of other European companies, Roland Petit's Ballet National de Marseille – a state company with a reputation for fine dancing and a fine theatrical energy – is admired, as is the Stuttgart Ballet, the creation of John Cranko, and still

Artists of the Nederlands Dans Theater in *Mutations*. This ballet
created a sensation when it was staged in 1970 because it showed
dancers performing in the nude, both on stage and in film clips which
were an integral part of the action. The choreography was by Glen
Tetley, and by Hans van Manen for the film sequences.

animated by the bright after-glow of his presence. Also in Germany, the Hamburg Ballet has a strong local following for its repertory of ballets by John Neumeier, its director and choreographer. The Dutch National Ballet offers an eclectic repertory, dominated by the work of three Dutch choreographers, Hans van Manen, Rudi van Dantzig and Toer van Schayk. The second Dutch company, Nederlands Dans Theater, has been notable for many years because of its exceptional creative record, with the idea of ten new ballets in a year no unusual feat — most other companies can muster three or four at best. Nederlands Dans Theater has made a positive policy of experimentation and after some dark years in which it opted for indifferent-to-tiresome American experimentation, it has won new acclaim with its audiences through the high-energy choreography of its present director, Jiři Kylian.

All these companies offer a sharply national view of ballet. It has been for a long time a cliché that ballet is 'international' art because it presents no language difficulties. But it is becoming increasingly evident that ballet speaks with strong national accents which are not necessarily comprehensible away from its native heath. What Germany finds modern, London and New York may find dated; what Paris thinks is chic is considered choreographic trumpery on Broadway; what London reveres as artistic innovation may be thought incomprehensible in Paris and New York; Balanchine's plot-less works, masterpieces to many, are anathema to others.

3

THE HISTORY OF BALLET

Dancing is no more than knowing how to bend and straighten the knees at the proper time.

Pierre Rameau, eighteenth century dancing master

The oldest ballets in the repertory today are those which date from the 1830s and 1840s, that golden age of the Romantic ballet when the ballerina emerged as the dominant figure in Western theatrical dance. There is one earlier surviving piece – *The Whims of Cupid and the Ballet Master* – which has been preserved by being continuously performed in the repertory of the Royal Danish Ballet ever since 1786, but it cannot be pretended that today its performance offers much indication of the style of dancing of the eighteenth century. In this, as with every ballet we have preserved from the nineteenth century, there have been massive amendments to choreographic text and style of performance brought by generations of dancers who have, understandably, introduced their own changes in order to up-date and revivify the works they perform. We meet here one of the great tragedies of ballet. For although performance manner has changed in music and in drama of past centuries there at least remains a printed and authentic text to which later performers must remain faithful. But ballet has not had a trustworthy and explicit method of notation (any system whereby dance can be written down) until recent times, and most particularly until the arrival of film and television, to ensure that what a choreographer has created can be seen in its original form. Hence our view of ballets of the past depends entirely upon a tradition of direct transmission from dancer to dancer across the years.

We can try to guess at the style of the dance and ballets of the eighteenth century and earlier from contemporary prints and technical manuals, but the theatre of the eighteenth century, for example, with its different lighting, with its absence of a curtain, with its vastly different traditions of performance and of costuming, inevitably means that the early achievements of ballet as an art are lost to us. It is as if we knew nothing of opera before Donizetti, nothing of drama before Victor Hugo. Nevertheless there exists sufficient testimony for us to sense that the ballets of the eighteenth century, and the court spectacles of an earlier age from which they sprang, were theatrically potent and immensely popular.

court ballet

It is convenient to see the first shoots of the theatrical form of dance in the splendid and varied entertainments which were part of the panoply of power of the Renaissance princes. By entertainments as different as water festivities, allegorical plays with their dance interludes, horse-ballets and those dazzling spectacles which combined song with dance, speech with machines that brought demons from Hell and divinities from Heaven, and even involved fireworks, the rulers of the Renaissance marked the great occasions of their lives. Royal births, marriages, treaties, all had their celebratory displays whose importance reflected upon the power and the wealth of the family concerned. Thus the great series of entertainments given by the Medici in Florence; thus, too, the tradition of the *ballet de cour* which emerged in the sixteenth-century French court of the Valois kings.

court ballet

The fact that the Medici Catherine was the wife of Henri II of France, and that three of her sons in turn succeeded to the throne, as Francois II, Charles IX and Henri III, while Catherine remained a potent force in the kingdom, must help account for the fact that the Italian traditions of court display became firmly implanted in the French court. Italian dancing-masters arrived to polish the performance technique of the courtiers, and to supervise the court displays by organising the dancers in evolutions (so that the actual social dance steps of the time became part of an elaborate sequence of patterns) and also to supervise the method of the entire production.

Two of these displays are especially significant. The *Ballet des Polonais* of 1573 was an hour-long spectacle staged

The entry for a herald and the one-legged drummers from the *Ballet des Fées des Forêts de St Germain*, a court ballet of 1625, which offered a series of extravagant scenes upon the theme of the qualities most sought after in a court gentleman.

In 1661, the Grand Duke Cosimo III of Tuscany married the youngest
daughter of Gaston d'Orléans, uncle of Louis XIV. The young bride's
arrival in Florence was the occasion of a tremendous procession and
horse ballet – *Il Mondo Festeggiante*.

in the Palace of the Tuileries in Paris to mark the arrival of
ambassadors from Poland to offer the throne of their country
to Catherine de' Medici's son, Henri d'Anjou. It presented the
edifying spectacle of a huge silvery rock being pushed into
the hall with sixteen of Catherine's court ladies perched on it.
After declaming Latin verse, they descended from the rock
and next moved through the careful patternings of a dance
which had been devised by the Queen's Italian *valet de chambre* and dancing master, Baldassarino di Belgiojoso, known
under his French name as Balthazar de Beaujoyeulx. They
gave each member of the royal party – in whose honour this
ballet ostensibly was – a gold plaque emblematic of the pro-
vinces of France. The implied comment in this entertainment
was that France would support at all times its Prince upon the
throne of Poland. Here we see very clearly the underlying
purpose – political – of so many of the court entertainments of
the time. Through symbol, allegory, metaphor, the political

message was decorated – but it was always understood. The **court** court entertainments presented throughout the courts of **ballet** Europe had this common attitude to greater or lesser extent.

De Beaujoyeulx was to be responsible for the greatest of these *ballets de cour.* This was *Le Ballet Comique de la Reine,* staged in 1581 in the Palace of the Louvre in Paris as part of two weeks of festivities to mark the union of the King's favourite, the Duc de Joyeuse, to the sister of his Queen, Louise. For five hours the members of the court were ranged in tiered stands along either side of the hall, and watched a dramatic entertainment whose purpose was to suggest that the political and religious strife so wounding to the nation might be healed, and that the monarch himself was stressing the support which the Catholic cause must expect from the throne. From ten at night until three the next morning the court enjoyed a spectacle which involved declamation, music provided by a band seated in carefully devised scenery, and the formal dances devised by de Beaujoyeulx to tell the story of Ulysses escaping from Circe's enchantments.

These court ballets had a focus, in that they were per-formed very directly towards a 'presence', which meant the monarch or prince or dedicatee of the entertainment – a fact which is clear from the inconography of the period. The 'choreography' resided in a skilled devising of shapes and patterns of movement ideally to be viewed from a raised position, whose floor plan contained the novelty of the entertainment since the steps were those of the differing social dances of the period. An interesting parallel can be made with the ballroom formation dancing so popular today, in which the steps are those prescribed for a given dance but 'choreographed' into patterns of considerable ingenuity.

The setting for these court ballets was, of course, the palace itself or, in fine weather, a courtyard or open space might serve. Decoration could range from the elaborate scenic effects which were so greatly admired in Florentine extrava-ganzas under the Medici – where complicated machinery allowed divinities to appear from the skies borne on clouds, and fireworks brought an entertainment to a fittingly blazing finale – to the smaller free-standing pieces of scenery in which nymphs or demons, or groups of musicians, were placed, as in

The Grand Carrousel took place in Paris to celebrate the birth of an heir to Louis XIV. Five squadrons of horsemen represented various nations. Above is the King's brother, Philippe d'Orléans, known as 'Monsieur', as the King of Persia.

Le Ballet Comique de la Reine of 1581. Decorated carts, splendid processions, water fêtes, mock battles and jousts, were all part of this paraphernalia of eye-catching splendour, and so, too, was the extreme complexity and brilliance of costuming. Engravings showing the members of Louis XIV's court (led by the monarch himself) in the great horse-ballet of 1662, *Le Grand Carrousel;* the engravings by the French artist Jacques Callot (1592–1635), showing court festivities in Italy, as well as

France; the existing designs by such great masters of Italian stage decoration as Stefano della Bella (1610–64); or the costuming and scenery designed by Inigo Jones for the court masques during the reign of Charles I (many in the collection of the Duke of Devonshire at Chatsworth), indicate the elaboration and extreme subtlety and beauty of design for court entertainments.

court ballet

From this high point under the Valois monarchs, French court ballet was to decline and alter, becoming less grand under Henri IV and Louis XIII, a fact dictated by both economic considerations and an inevitable change of taste. The final burst of grandeur of the court ballet was to come with Louis XIV. As part of the apparatus of splendour and luxury which surrounded Le Grand Monarque there emerged a tradition of exceptionally brilliant court entertainments in which the young King was to participate until his early thirties. The King loved dancing. His appearance in such works as *Le Ballet Royal de la Nuit* enhanced his identity in the eyes of the court as a Sun, for the King habitually appeared in such roles as Apollo and the Sun God whose rays could be beneficent or scorching. Such exceptional entertainments as the horse-ballet of 1662, *Le Grand Carrousel*, which celebrated the birth of the Dauphin, and *Les Plaisirs de l'Ile Enchantée*, which occupied three days in May 1664 at Versailles in dance, processions, banquets and drama (Molière wrote *La Princesse d'Elide* for the occasion) were typical. The latter entertainment was ostensibly given in honour of the Queen and the Queen Mother, but everyone was aware that the true dedicatee was the young King's adorable mistress Mademoiselle de la Vallière. The final moment of *Les Plaisirs* came with the superb firework display which marked the destruction of the Palace of Alcina.

The importance of dancing as an activity for the nobility cannot be over-stressed. From the middle of the fifteenth century we have evidence in dance manuals, and every other form of visual record, of the attraction and significance of dance in the life of the aristocracy. While the King or ruling Prince danced in spectacles or patronised and encouraged them, participation of courtiers was central to all forms of court divertissements.

opera–ballet

It is significant that when Louis XIV abandoned dancing as a performer at the end of the 1660s – though his love of it had already been manifest in the establishing of the Académie Royale de Danse in 1661 in Paris – dance was given an added impetus in its move into the theatre. This move was associated with the emergent form of the opera-ballet under the Italian Jean Baptiste Lully (1632–87). Lully, born in Florence, came to France and appeared first as dancer and then became a favoured musician of Louis XIV. A man of considerable ability, and eager for power, he secured for himself the essential royal *privilège* (licence) for the performance of opera from its first beneficiaries and thereafter, through the establishing of the Académie Royale de Musique in 1671, Lully was to become the dominant influence upon the operatic stagings with their interpolated dance interludes.

The dance academy was to prove impotent: it consisted initially of dancing-masters concerned with codifying court and social dance. It was the activities of the music academy, later to be known simply as the Paris Opéra, which fostered the professional aspects of ballet as a theatrical form.

It was at the Opéra in 1681 that the first professional female dancers made their appearance. (They were Mlles Lafontaine, Fanon, Lepeintre and Roland.) In 1713 a school of dancing was officially established to regularise the supply of dancers for the opera-ballets which were by now a staple fare of the lyric theatre.

But for all the richness of musical and decorative collaboration, the French opera-ballet was essentially hidebound in its reliance upon formal attitudes already well established. The opera-ballet had advanced not at all in expressive power or truth since the genre had been established by Lully. Performance manner became more brilliant; the collaboration of the finest decorators produced stage pictures of great elegance, and under Jean-Philippe Rameau the score reached an apogee of musical distinction, in such works as his *Les Indes Galantes* of 1735. But the dance relied entirely upon virtuosity on already well-known lines: elegance and grace of manner, superb deportment, brilliance – for the men – of footwork, and

A design for a fiery spirit in an opera-ballet of the mid-eighteenth century. The male dancer is wearing a tonnelet, that hooped skirt which could extend to the width of his arms. The decoration of flames in the costume made his identity very clear to the audiences at that time.

opera–ballet   distinction and grace for the women. But their costuming was basically the broad and encumbering skirt, the panniers, feathers and predictable decorations for the ballerinas, and later the tonnelet (that hooped and wired skirt which extended at thigh level to the width of the danseur's arms) for the man. The opera-ballet combined sung and danced scenes, but the dance was no more than a divertissement illustrating some moment in the action established by the singers: it neither developed the drama nor ventured beyond the formal display of the dancers' virtuosity and distinction of manner. There was no drama, no emotion other than that of display. The most interesting artistic development in professional theatrical dancing in the early eighteenth century lies in the quest for a performance manner more expressive and more truthfully dramatic.

the ballet d'action

This development in theatrical dancing can be observed in the work in London of the English dancing-master John Weaver (1673–1760). Weaver was fascinated by the ideas which he culled from his reading of classic Greek and Latin texts, in which he learned of the expressive performances by mimes. Thus he set about staging his 'pantomimes' in which he sought to present a dramatic narrative through mime and dance. In 1717 his *Loves of Mars and Venus* was a wordless performance in which one of the greatest French dancers, Le Grand Dupré (1697–1774), appeared with the English actress and dancer Hester Santlow. Weaver was a prolific writer and theorist about dancing and his books and choreographies must be seen as an essential contribution to the development of the *ballet d'action,* that narrative dance entertainment.

The idea of expressive mime was not exclusive to Weaver. Three years before *The Loves of Mars and Venus* the Duchesse du Maine had invited two leading dancers from the Paris Opéra, Jean Balon and Françoise Prévost, to mime part of the fourth act of Corneille's tragedy, *Les Horaces,* as part of a series of entertainments which she was giving at her Château at Sceaux.

The desire for a greater naturalism was also a quality associated with one of the two great French ballerinas of the early eighteenth century. Marie Sallé (1707–56), a pupil of Prévost, made her début at the Paris Opéra in 1721 and won great acclaim. But it was a performance in London in 1734 in her own ballet, *Pygmalion,* which suggested something of her aspirations for her art. She reformed her costuming, preferring naturally dressed hair to the elaborate coiffure more usual on the stage, and a Grecian simplicity of costume as opposed to the wide and cumbersome skirts which were the female dancer's habitual dress. If Sallé sought some greater freedom of expressive manner, her great rival Marie Camargo (1710–70) endeared herself to the public through the lightness and vivacity of her dance style. The reform in dress which she initiated reflected her virtuosity: she dared to shorten her skirts sufficiently to reveal the pretty brilliance of her footwork – she is credited with being able to perform *entrechat quatre.*

But the great reforms necessary to free dance itself from the rigid formulae of opera-ballet were those associated with the writings and the creations of Jean-Georges Noverre.

Noverre did not invent the idea of the *ballet d'action* but it is to him that we look for the best indications of the desire for a more truthful and expressive form of dance in the theatre. Born in Paris in 1727, Noverre was a dancer and choreographer who early became disenchanted with the rigid attitudes of the theatre dance of his time. In 1760 he published his *Lettres sur la danse et les ballets,* which offer an exceptional view of the state of dance in the mid-eighteenth century and a no less convincing set of precepts (many of them valid still today) aimed at the reform of theatrical dance. Noverre inveighed against technical brilliance when it sacrificed expressive power. He made mockery of costuming and masks which disguised the identity of dancers and encumbered them with wigs, panniers and the preposterous tonnelet.

He declared: 'Let us have less of the fairy tale, less of the marvellous, more truth and more realism, and dancing will appear to much greater advantage.' Elsewhere he wrote, 'Everything will speak, each movement will be expressive, each attitude will depict a particular situation, each gesture will reveal a thought, each glance will convey a new sentiment;

the
ballet
d'action

69

La Camargo. This enchanting painting by Lancret is in the Wallace Collection, London.

everything will be captivating because all will be a true and faithful imitation of nature.'

In the year in which he published his *Lettres*, Noverre became ballet master in Stuttgart, the seat of one of the most extraordinary rulers in Europe, the theatre-loving Grand Duke Karl Eugen. For seven years Noverre produced a series of magnificent ballets on the conventional heroic themes of his time, which employed some of the finest dancers in Europe to scores provided by the usual Italian composers of the period. Although nothing remains of his choreography, his influence was inevitably to be felt and to be spread by example and by report around Europe.

In 1767 Noverre moved to Vienna. In that city he became associated with Gluck, whose reforms of opera were no less significant than Noverre's ideals for ballet. But Noverre's aim was always to become director of the ballet at the Paris Opéra, and he achieved this in 1776. But although protected by Queen Marie Antoinette's patronage, his Opéra years were stormy. He had been imposed upon the theatre,

This caricature by J. Cruickshank of 1798 relates to the scandal when it was thought that the French dancers appearing in London were too immodest in their dress. Bishop Barrington of Durham declared that the dancers were emissaries of the French Government sent to undermine morals and encourage divorce.

and this fact produced a mistrust and active dislike of him which led to his being forced to resign in 1781. His subsequent career brought him to London, where he had already appeared and staged ballets, and had made a friend of David Garrick; but the end of his life was spent in retirement in France where he died in 1810. Though not the inventor of the *ballet d'action*, Noverre is its most important advocate through his writings, and his influence can be seen as central to the emergence of a theatrically truthful style of ballet at this time.

By Noverre's time dance technique had produced generations of dancers of remarkable virtuosity and bravura. Chief among these was the great Gaetano Vestris (1729–1808), known with some justification to his public as the God of the Dance. Gaetano, the darling of Europe and arrogant as such fame inevitably made him, was the outstanding exponent of the 'noble' or 'serious' style. His son by the dancer Marie Allard, Auguste Vestris (1760–1842), was less handsome than his father, less imposing in stature, and therefore destined to the *demi-caractère* style. (Dancers at this time were rigidly categorised according to physique and temperament – the third style, the 'comic', was inferior to the *demi-caractère* – but although the formal categories ended at the beginning of the nineteenth century the sort of dancers and the attitudes attaching to the old descriptions still apply even today.)

Auguste Vestris represents a vital bridge between the dance of the eighteenth century and the Romantic age which was to flourish in ballet by the 1830s. Through his training from his father he was heir to the greatest traditions of the eighteenth-century noble style. His own style, though, had been developed; his brilliance as a dancer in the *demi-caractère* style led him to disregard and combine the previously rigid rules of the three styles and his dance was acknowledged as both more exciting and 'newer' than that of any other dancer. It is most significant that on his retirement from dancing he became a teacher and passed on to his two best pupils, Jules Perrot and August Bournonville, the style he himself had evolved. Perrot and Bournonville were the two greatest choreographers of the Romantic Age.

Auguste Vestris dancing in London in 1781. The exuberance and
charm of his style is clear in this caricature, as is the fact that he and
his father, Gaetano, were immensely well paid. His hat is full of bank
notes, and he holds a purse labelled 'English guineas'.

73

romantic ballet

Romanticism triumphed at the Paris Opéra in 1832 with the staging of Filippo Taglioni's *La Sylphide*. It was this ballet which swept away the dry and by now dusty attitudes of the academic dance which had been preserved at the Opéra under the long régime of Pierre Gardel, ballet-master and choreographer at that theatre from 1787 until his retirement in 1829.

La Sylphide must be seen as the culmination of a movement to humanise and expand the range of choreography which had begun with the work of Noverre. Noverre's pupil Jean Dauberval (1742–1806) had suggested in his *La Fille mal gardée* of 1789 how the lives of simple folk could be translated to the ballet stage. Charles Louis Didelot (1767–1837) was another crucial figure much influenced by Noverre. In London in 1796 he staged his most famous ballet, *Flore et Zéphire*, in which dancers were made to fly by means of wires. For some thirty years subsequently in Russia he produced a series of beautiful and influential ballets which developed the Noverrean theories. In Milan, Salvatore Viganò (1769–1821) was a dancer greatly influenced by Dauberval, and for the last ten years of his life he produced a series of immense dance dramas at the Teatro alla Scala which offered complex narrative told largely in mime and rhythmic movement. The activities of all these choreographers must be seen as indicating how the ballet world was preparing itself for its next great development.

Romanticism was by now entirely established in all the arts of the day – we have but to think of Berlioz' *Symphonie Fantastique*, the paintings of Géricault, the poetry of Lamartine. It was the début at the Paris Opéra in 1827 of Marie Taglioni which initiated the new image of dancing. Born in 1804, daughter of the Italian ballet-master Filippo Taglioni and his Swedish wife, Marie must at first have seemed unpromising material for the dance career to which her father destined her. A thin, long-limbed child, she was placed by her father with fine teachers in Paris, but when he summoned her to Vienna (where he was then ballet-master) in 1822 to make her début he took charge of her training him-

self. A period of gruelling exercises, sometimes for up to six
hours a day, were to transform the gifted girl into a unique performer. Her thinness was to be etherealised into an airy lightness. Her somewhat prim features were to be softened by a gentle smile. Her long arms would be curved and crossed in poses of beguiling grace; a technical mastery would be encouraged, as a result of the long sweated hours of study, which would give her a prowess that needed no support from a danseur and no other justification save a floating and delicious ease. By the time she came to make her début in Paris in 1827, in an interpolated *pas* in the opera *Le Sicilien,* Marie Taglioni was a radically new type of dancer.

Her impact was immediate. Every other dancer sought to copy her style – the verb *Taglioniser,* 'to dance like Taglioni', entered the language of the Opéra – and she consolidated her position in 1831 with her appearance in the ballet of the nuns in Meyerbeer's opera *Robert the Devil.*

In this scene, a group of ghostly nuns led by their abbess (Taglioni) rose from their graves and danced a wild bacchanal in the cloisters of a ruined abbey. (There is a Degas painting of this scene, though of a later production.) The installation of gas lighting at the Paris Opéra made possible effects of mystery and moonlight. The white-clad figures drifting phantom-like through the night seemed an image implicit with Romantic fantasy. The tenor in this opera, Adolphe Nourrit, conceived an idea of a ballet in which Taglioni might seem yet again a creature from another world. He spoke of this to Marie's choreographer father, and a year later the full impact of Romanticism was felt in ballet with the first performance of *La Sylphide.*

In it the Romantic age's concern with dreams of the unattainable, and a kind of feverish poetry which embraced both exotic location and unrestrained passions, were all given extraordinary expression in the story of a young Scottish farmer James, who is lured from his wedding day by the attractions of the sylphide. He endeavours to possess her, but at the end of the ballet the sylphide is dead and he has lost both his ideal and his human love. In *La Sylphide* the entire machinery of the Romantic ballet can be seen. It stressed the dominance of the female dancer; its setting was – for the time

– exotic and remote. It allowed for an unprecedented expression of emotion; it typified the Romantic quest for flight from reality.

In the performance of Marie Taglioni we find an identity for the ballerina which, amazingly, persists to this day. Taglioni revealed qualities of lightness, grace and decorum which were largely unknown to previous ballerinas. In her use of pointe work she offered an artistic and dramatically cogent use of a newly discovered extension of the female dancer's technique whereby, despite very light slippers which gave little support to the feet, the ballerina rose on the tip of her toes to hold momentary poses suggestive of flight. The Romantic invasion of the air – suggested by Didelot's *Flore et Zéphire* – had begun.

With Taglioni came the emergence of the ballerina as the central figure of dancing in the theatre, a state of affairs which has lasted almost until our own time. The male dancer – dominant throughout the eighteenth century – was now to start to be relegated to that ignoble role of fetching and carrying the female dancer, and keeping well out of the way when dancing itself took place. This role was to be his in almost every centre of dance save Copenhagen, for the rest of the century. In Copenhagen, August Bournonville, dancer of great talent as well as choreographer of genius, was able to maintain a proper balance between the sexes in his ballets, developing male technique from his schooling with Auguste Vestris to produce the beautiful and elegant male style by which Danish dancers are still recognised.

But for the audience of the Romantic age – and thereafter – the ballerina *was* ballet. That she was also, as she had been in the eighteenth century, a figure of moral ambivalence, often thought to be no more than a loose-living object for any man rich enough to buy her, is part of the regrettable tradition of sexual opportunism that surrounded the female dancer. At the Paris Opéra, the corps de ballet and the leading ballerinas were part of a market in bodies which was an

Right: Marie Taglioni as the Sylphide. This engraving conveys everything that the audience adored in her delicate grace, an illusion of weightlessness, and a manner both beguiling and demure.

Fanny Elssler as Esmeralda in Perrot's ballet of that name, from a painting by Paul Bürde dated 1849.

accepted fact of the dancer's life. Girls were encouraged to take up dancing as an escape both from the harshness of metropolitan labour and as a chance to find a rich protector or to form a series of financially rewarding liaisons. They were part of a social and sexual order which expected them to be little better than prostitutes. The male dancer was to become a creature beneath consideration. 'We have nearly banished him from the stage', noted one critic in the 1840s, and there was a serious attempt to rid the Opéra company of men during the latter part of the century. And this attitude was to prevail well into the twentieth century.

With *La Sylphide* Marie Taglioni became, and remained for the next fifteen years of her career, the supreme embodiment of the Romantic dance. She had rivals – notably Fanny Elssler (1810–84), the Austrian-born virtuoso whose art was in direct opposition to that of Taglioni. Théophile Gautier, the French poet and the best commentator on the Romantic dance, summed up the difference in his celebrated dictum 'Taglioni is a Christian dancer – Elssler a pagan'. In Elssler's dancing the audience saw a warmth, a vivacity, and a dramatic power and temperament which beguiled them utterly. Her most celebrated solo was the Spanish-style *Cachucha,* but her greatness is more truly recorded in her triumphs as the tragic heroine of *Giselle* and in *La Gypsy.* Like the other ballerinas of the period she travelled widely, triumphing both in the United States, where Congress adjourned early in order to attend her performance, and in Russia, where her farewell performances in Moscow were greeted with 300 bouquets, 42 curtain calls and that classic accolade, when the horses were unhitched from her carriage and replaced by adoring young men who pulled the carriage from the theatre to an hotel where a banquet was given in her honour.

We sense in the peregrinations of Elssler something of the wide-spread popularity which ballet had now attained: Elssler danced throughout Europe and the New World, from Vienna to Moscow, from London to Cuba. Nor were her colleagues and successors strangers to travel: the ballet *Giselle* was first presented in Paris in 1841. Within a decade it had been produced in Bordeaux, Marseille, London, Vienna, St Petersburg, Lyons, Milan, Venice, Berlin, Dublin, Lisbon,

Moscow, Madrid, The Hague, Stockholm, Rome, Boston, New York, Philadelphia, Charleston, New Orleans, Barcelona, Copenhagen, with a variety of ballerinas. Throughout Europe, across the extent of the Austro-Hungarian Empire, and in the Imperial theatres of Tsarist Russia, ballet knew great popularity and the dancers of the nineteenth century, despite the difficulties of travel, danced and moved on, just as their forbears in the eighteenth century had done.

Three of the most famous ballerinas of the Romantic era were each involved in a relationship with a leading choreographer of the age. Carlotta Grisi (1819–99) was a member of the celebrated Italian musical family – her sisters and cousins being great singers. As a young dancer in Naples she was discovered by Jules Perrot and became his pupil and mistress. Perrot (1810–92) had started his career in the popular theatres of his time dancing eccentric roles as a boy performer. He studied with Auguste Vestris whose training transformed him into an outstanding virtuoso dancer: between 1830 and 1835 as a principal dancer at the Paris Opéra Perrot danced with Taglioni, rivalling her in airy brilliance so that he was called 'Taglioni's dancing brother'. But the decline in popularity of the male dancer, and Taglioni's reluctance to share public acclaim, set Perrot on an itinerant course through Europe and brought him to the meeting with Grisi in 1836. They danced together throughout Europe, Perrot shaping her gifts, and eventually in 1840 they arrived in Paris where they made a reasonable impression in an operetta at a boulevard theatre. Circumstances resulted in an engagement for Carlotta Grisi to dance at the Opéra – though Perrot, who had hoped to return to his parent theatre, was excluded – and in 1841 the production of *Giselle* brought Grisi to vast public acclaim. This central masterpiece of the balletic age again offers the two sides of Romantic dance's coin: the first act set in a Rhineland village, in which the heroine is betrayed, the second act located in the moonlit glades of a midnight forest where vengeful spirits of girls seek to dance the hero to his death while the ghost of Giselle endeavours to sustain him.

Although the ballet was choreographed by Jean Coralli, chief ballet-master at the Opéra, it is known that Perrot devised the superlative dances for Grisi and for Lucien Petipa

Carlotta Grisi in the second act of *Giselle*. A thoroughly idealised
portrait, it nevertheless conveys what the Romantic audience
thought it saw: the ghostly, hovering and alluring figure of the Wili.

as the hero. Grisi's career thereafter found her dancing through Europe and finally in Russia, to great acclaim until her retirement in 1853.

Perrot, disappointed in his hopes in Paris, was invited to London where, between 1842 and 1848, he staged a most important series of ballets at Her Majesty's Theatre. These are among the great masterpieces of the Romantic *ballet d'action*, works notable for their theatrical energy as for their choreographic beauty: *Ondine, La Esmeralda, Caterina, Lalla Rookh, Eoline* among them. Perrot is also remembered as the choreographer of the celebrated *Pas de Quatre* of 1845 in which the astute theatrical manager Benjamin Lumley brought together four of the divinities of this golden age: Taglioni, Grisi, Fanny Cerrito and Lucile Grahn. In 1848 Perrot left London for a decade in St Petersburg as principal dancer and choreographer. Here he gave the Imperial Russian Ballet a priceless inheritance of his greatest ballets. On his return from Russia in 1859 he found the ballet world sadly changed and the art of choreography in a decline: the heyday of the Romantic ballet in Western Europe ended as its first star ballerinas retired from the stage, and public taste swung away from dance and was stimulated by the glories of opera and opera singing in the mid-nineteenth century. Perrot taught at the Opéra (he can be seen in several Degas drawings and paintings) and retired to the country where he died in 1892.

Fanny Cerrito (1817–1909) was born in Naples where she made her début in 1832. A dancer of exceptional sparkle and elevation, she was the darling of London and it was here that she enjoyed triumphs in such ballets as *Ondine* and *La Vivandière*. She was also a choreographer, and married a choreographer, Arthur St Léon (1821–70). Cerrito went with her husband to Paris in 1847 where he became a choreographer at the Opéra and she danced; she went with success to St Petersburg and Moscow into the 1850s, but by then she had separated from St Léon and during her fifty-two years in retirement she lived quietly in Paris. She died in the month that saw the Paris appearance of the Diaghilev Ballet with *Les Sylphides*, that innovatory work which looked back to the style of which Cerrito had been so illustrious an exponent.

Arthur St Léon, famous as dancer, choreographer and

Three of the chief divinities of the Romantic Age: Fanny Cerrito,
Marie Taglioni and Lucile Grahn, surrounding Arthur St Léon in the
Pas des Déesses from Perrot's *The Judgment of Paris* in 1846.

violinist, travelled through Europe and finally succeeded Perrot as first ballet-master in St Petersburg. For a decade he produced a series of major works there, also contriving to mount ballets at the Paris Opéra during the summer months when the Imperial theatres were closed. In the last year of his life he was supervising the ballet by which his name is now remembered: *Coppélia,* staged at the Paris Opéra in 1870 and seeming the last flicker of the Romantic dance.

The fourth member of the *Pas de Quatre,* Lucile Grahn, was born in Copenhagen in 1819. Her training she owed entirely to August Bournonville. This other great choreographer of the Romantic age was born of a French ballet-master father, Antoine, and a Swedish mother, but he was proudly Danish and equally proudly a dancer. The vital years of his training were spent in Paris under Auguste Vestris. In 1830 he assumed the directorship of the Royal Danish Ballet, by then a moribund company. His achievement between that date and 1877 when he retired was to create a magnificent dance style, a magnificent repertory and a climate of artistic and moral dignity markedly in contrast to the balletic traditions in the rest of Europe. Bournonville thought Marie Taglioni his 'ideal dancer' and it was in her image that he sought to shape his young pupil Grahn, whom he also loved. For Grahn he decided to stage his own version of *La Sylphide* and it is this staging which survives to this day. Grahn could not reciprocate Bournonville's feelings and she left Denmark in 1839 and shone thereafter on the international scene, dancing in Paris, London and St Petersburg. In 1856 she ended her dancing career and became a ballet-mistress. Her latter years were spent in Munich, where she had married an Austrian tenor, and she is remembered today also as the choreographer for some of Wagner's operas in their first Bayreuth stagings.

Bournonville's ballets were carefully preserved in Copenhagen and have been treated as a priceless heritage by the Danes. Thus, today, the Royal Danish Ballet can offer a dozen works by the great choreographer which afford us an incomparable insight into the ballet of the nineteenth century. Such masterworks as *Napoli, A Folk Tale, Kermesse in Bruges, Konservatoriet* and *La Sylphide* reveal Bournonville as a choreographer who preserved and embellished the honourable status of the male dancer and who inculcated in his artists a tradition of dramatic veracity which means that today Copenhagen-trained dancers are still masters of a beautiful technical manner and of powerful mime.

the Imperial Russian Ballet

Although the Romantic ballet in Western Europe fell into a decline by the middle of the nineteenth century, it was to flourish in St Petersburg and be carried forward in the second half of the nineteenth century under the guidance of Marius Petipa. Theatrical dancing in Russia was a development which owed everything to the Empress Anna Ivanovna, who encouraged the founding, in 1738, of a school in St Petersburg for the education of children of palace servants to become dance pupils. Thereafter a ballet company was initiated which owed its increasing distinction to a series of ballet-masters from France, Italy and Austria. The great developments of the nineteenth-century Russian dance are owed to a series of French ballet-masters, beginning with Didelot who arrived in 1801, and continuing with a French ballet-master, Alexis Blache, then a German, Antoine Titus, and then Perrot and St Léon.

Marius Petipa, born in 1818 into a family of French dancers – his father Jean was a ballet-master who eventually became a teacher at the school in St Petersburg – arrived in St Petersburg in 1847 as premier danseur. He spent the ten years of Perrot's reign as dancer, absorbing from that great master of the *ballet d'action* a clear understanding of the dramatic possibilities of ballet. Though he inevitably aspired to the post of first ballet-master, he had to wait until St Léon's years as first ballet-master for some success as a choreographer. This came in 1862 when he knew extreme success with his first full-length ballet, *La Fille du Pharaon*. It was followed by other ballets and, with St Léon's departure in 1869, Petipa's appointment as first ballet-master. During the next three decades it was Petipa who was responsible for the flood of grand spectacular ballets, complex full-length extravaganzas which made such tremendous use of the outstanding dancers produced by the Imperial school in St Petersburg. It was during these years that Italian virtuoso ballerinas were the added stimulus for public interest in performance. In Italy itself a very fine teaching tradition, particularly notable in Milan under Carlo Blasis, was producing magnificent and technically brilliant ballerinas, with very strong 'pointes', though there was little choreography of merit to display them. Hence, Italian ballerinas were sought throughout Europe as visiting stars. A fashion in Italy for extravagant full-length dance spectacles like Manzotti's *Excelsior* was a parallel but much less interesting activity to Petipa's great creations in St Petersburg.

Vitally important among the Italian ballerinas was Virginia Zucchi (1849–1930). A dancer of extreme dramatic power, Zucchi was to have a profound influence upon Russian ballet. In the late 1880s a series of guest performances in St Petersburg and Moscow revitalised the audience's interest in the art of ballet through the intensity and passionate involvement of her performances. It is worth noting that her appearances were to stimulate the sensibilities of the Russian artist and man of the theatre Alexandre Benois (1870–1960) and to inspire in him an enthusiasm which he would in due time pass on to the young Serge Diaghilev; Zucchi also stimulated in the dancers of the period a greater appreciation of the dramatic potential of ballet. In her memoirs the outstanding ballerina M. F. Kshessinskaya (1872–1971) paid special tribute to this fact.

The Italian invasion continued to the end of the century, its most notable figures being Pierina Legnani (1863–1923), who astounded St Petersburg with her *fouettés,* a fact immortalised in Petipa's third act of *Swan Lake;* Carlotta Brianza (1867–1930), the first Aurora in *The Sleeping Beauty;* and in Enrico Cecchetti (1850–1928), whose technical brilliance was matched by a comparable dramatic skill, both these facets celebrated in his creations of the Blue Bird and the evil fairy Carabosse in *The Sleeping Beauty* in 1890.

The development of a 'Russian' style of dancing at this time evolved through the effect upon a basically French school – that of Perrot and Petipa – burnished by the example of Italianate virtuosity and by Cecchetti's teaching, to which must be added the marked influence of Christian Johansson (1817–1903). This Swedish dancer studied under August Bournonville. In quest of engagements he danced in St Petersburg and in 1841 partnered Taglioni in her Russian appearances. In that year he was admitted into the Imperial Ballet, married a Russian, adopted Russian nationality, and was first a premier danseur of noblest style, and then from 1860 onwards, a prodigious teacher. It is to him that Russia owes the Bournonville development of the French style and a continued respect for male dancing. Johansson's pupils, notably Nicholas Legat and A. Y. Vaganova, were to be very important in perpetuating and extending this style and also in shaping the emergent Russian style of the latter years of the century.

Although Petipa starred Italian virtuosos in his ballets there was a no less important galaxy of Russian ballerinas from Yelena Andreyanova (1819–57), the first Russian Giselle, and Martha Muravieva (1838–79) to Ekaterina Vazem (1848–1937), who was Petipa's favourite ballerina. It was for Vazem that Petipa was to produce one of his grandest works, *La Bayadère* (1877), which is one of the few remaining Petipa ballets to be seen today. Of the massive output of this greatest of nineteenth-century choreographers little remains. Each year he had to produce a new spectacle at the beginning of the season, which would serve to beguile the aristocratic audience at the Bolshoy Theatre in St Petersburg – the ballet company only moved to the Maryinsky Theatre in 1886. Inevitably the extent of his output meant that many of Petipa's major works have been lost. However *La Bayadère, The Sleeping Beauty,* and *Raymonda* of 1898 (despite its idiotic story) are testimony to his genius. In one other Petipa ballet, *Swan Lake* of 1895, which he composed jointly with Lev Ivanov, the second ballet-master in St Petersburg, there survives – in the rare authentic productions today – remarkable evidence of the emotional power of the great creations of the Imperial Ballet.

Swan Lake was probably guaranteed survival, as was *The Sleeping Beauty* and Ivanov's *The Nutcracker,* by the magnificence of the Tchaikovsky scores. Traditionally the ballet music was little more than agreeable accompaniment to

the
Imperial
Russian
Ballet

the dancing provided by such official purveyors of ballet scores as Cesare Pugni and Ludwig Minkus. Their music was often charming and always danceable. It was the genius of Tchaikovsky, and later of Glazunov, which opened new horizons of theatrical grandeur for ballet music, as in Paris had Léo Delibes (to whom Tchaikovsky acknowledged indebtedness). But by the end of the nineteenth century it must be seen that the ageing Petipa, though still producing masterpieces, was producing masterpieces of rigid and hidebound predictability. A young dancer, Mikhail Fokine (1880–1942) entered the Imperial Ballet as a first soloist in 1898. He was appalled and distressed by what he saw as the sterility and artificiality of the repertory he was called upon to dance. In his memoirs he calls the chapter about his early years in the ballet at the Maryinsky Theatre 'Beginning of Service, and Disappointments, in the Ballet'.

4

BALLET IN THE TWENTIETH CENTURY

The dance belongs to the kingdom of the imagination and finds its images in it.

August Bournonville

Mikhail Fokine

By 1904 Fokine had alread formulated theories about changes he thought necessary in the Imperial Russian Ballet. He sent a libretto for a ballet on the theme of Daphnis and Chloë to the Director of the Imperial Theatres, together with an introduction in which he proposed certain essential reforms in the ballet – reforms which make him seem like a latter-day Noverre. In brief, he declared that ballets on historical subjects should be true, in period movement and in design – a far cry from the universal tutu and pointe shoes which were the dress of ballerinas whether they were meant to be ancient Egyptian princesses, fairies or gypsies. Music, design, mime, should all seek expressive truth and aim at forming a cohesive whole rather than making a succession of bravura numbers which opted for display. Fokine began as a choreographer by staging short ballets for the pupils he taught at the Imperial School. Between 1905 and 1908 he succeeded in putting some of his ideas into practice in a series of works produced for his pupils, for private performances and eventually for the Imperial Ballet.

It is a comment on prevailing conditions that his ballet *Eunice* of 1907 needed dancers to appear barefoot on the stage. But bare legs and feet were forbidden on the illustrious boards of the Maryinsky, and so dancers had to wear flesh-coloured tights and paint toes upon them. *Eunice* is significant in that for the first time dancers appeared credibly like the historical characters they were supposed to represent. In the same year Fokine was to collaborate with Alexandre Benois, who was designer and librettist for *Le Pavillon d'Armide*, a one-act ballet with music by Tcherepnin. It was through this collaboration that Fokine was introduced into the most influential artistic circle in St Petersburg which had as its focus Serge Diaghilev.

Serge Diaghilev

Born in 1872 in Perm, the son of a prosperous family of the provincial nobility, Serge Diaghilev was sent at the age of eighteen to St Petersburg to study law. He stayed with his cousins the Filosofov family, and through one cousin, Dima Filosofov, became involved in a group of young intellectuals. The group included Alexandre Benois, and, later, his friend the Jewish painter Léon Bakst, and Walter Nouvel, a young man much interested in music. Their close friendship and constant discussions about the arts were an important part of Diaghilev's artistic education, turning him from a provincial youth of raw energies into a far more polished figure, with broad artistic horizons. Diaghilev was first interested in music. The failure of his aspirations as a composer – Rimsky Korsakov had dismissed his pretensions – led him into a closer relationship with Benois and Bakst and the decision to involve himself more deeply in the world of art. There followed his

Serge Diaghilev as a young man in St Petersburg, drawn by his friend Valentin Serov. The white lock in his hair earned him the nick-name Chinchilla.

first tentative attempts at staging small exhibitions, beginning with water colours by British and German artists in 1895, gradually developing into a taste for showing something of the new art of Europe to St Petersburg. As part of his proselytising came the foundation of a magazine, appropriately enough called *The World of Art (Mir Isskustva)* which first appeared in 1898, of which he was editor-in-chief. It was this magazine, coupled with the continuing tradition of exhibitions, which was to show Diaghilev as a now influential figure in a new wave of artistic feelings in St Petersburg. Diaghilev was briefly involved with the Imperial Theatres in a projected staging of Delibes' *Sylvia,* for which his artist friends would provide designs, but Diaghilev's association with young artists was to rally the conservative forces within the theatre, and they succeeded in engineering his dismissal.

In 1905 Diaghilev presented a final exhibition in St Petersburg – of Russian historical portraits. In this year of the first revolution a reassessment of Russian painting might have seemed a retrograde step, but for Diaghilev it was a moment for pause and for considering the past because, as he said in a speech at the banquet which initiated the exhibition, '. . . we live in a terrible period of transition. We are doomed to die to pave the way for the resurrection of a new culture . . . We are witnesses of the greatest moment of summing up in history, in the name of a new and unknown culture, which will be created by us and which will also sweep us away.' (The whole text of this speech can be found in Arnold Haskell's *Diaghileff,* London 1935, the first and best biography of the great man, by one who knew him and who wrote it in collaboration with Walter Nouvel.)

Ballet Russe

At this moment Diaghilev decided to turn his attention to Europe, and there followed a series of enterprises which culminate in the Russian seasons of opera and ballet which were to revolutionise ballet in the West. In Paris in 1906 he arranged the vastly successful exhibition of Russian art at the Grand Palais. In 1907 there came the concerts of Russian music in Paris which involved Glazunov, Rachmaninov, Arthur Nikisch and Scriabin, and, very significantly, a concert performance of an operatic scene by the great basso Feodor Chaliapine. Chaliapine's success as a singer of genius who was also an actor of genius led to an invitation to bring a complete opera to Paris in 1908. Thus a brand new staging of *Boris Godunov* by Mussorgsky was prepared under Diaghilev's supervision, its decoration by Russian artists far more beautiful and vivid than any native Russian production, with Chaliapine in the title role. *Boris* was a triumph at the Paris Opéra, and there came the decision for an extended season in the following year which would include several operas and also bring the Russian Ballet to Paris.

Five operas were scheduled, together with some ballet programmes which would show Paris something of an art which Russians knew Paris had lost. But royal patronage was necessary and when the Grand Duke Vladimir who was to have backed the season died, Diaghilev had to reduce his operatic presentations to one work, *Ivan the Terrible*, with acts from *Prince Igor* and *Russlan and Ludmilla*, which would be shown in tandem with ballet. So on 18 May 1909, a *répétition générale* took place at the Théâtre du Châtelet of a programme of ballets and one act from *Prince Igor*.

In this performance we see the effective re-birth of ballet as a theatrical spectacle and a serious art form in the West. It is significant that the directors of the Paris Opéra found it inconceivable to lend their theatre for a largely balletic season: hence Diaghilev took over an old melodrama house, redecorated and refurbished it with characteristic extravagance for his month's season. What *le tout Paris* saw at the Théâtre du Châtelet was the triumphant assertion of ballet as an art.

The greatest success at the first night was the Polovtsian Dances which accompanied the single act of *Prince Igor* that was shown. Newly choreographed by Mikhail Fokine for the season, they filled the stage with a horde of Tartar warriors led by Adolph Bolm in dances of barbaric energy. The impact of these dances and these male dancers was tremendous: as Serge Grigoriev, Diaghilev's right-hand man for the entire twenty years of the Russian Ballet's existence, records in his very sober and truthful chronicle *The Diaghilev Ballet 1909–1929* (London 1953): 'The pandemonium was indescribable.' And the evening 'marked a resurrection of the ballet in the world outside Russia'. This was due not just to the undoubted virility of the Russian men; it was an artistry in design, a choreographic genius, and the technique and expressiveness of such dancers as Tamara Karsavina, Anna Pavlova and Vaslav Nijinsky which turned all Paris into the adoring slaves

**Ballet
Russe**

of the Russian dancers. Fokine's genius revealed new vistas of balletic beauty. His works comprised the repertory: *Le Pavillion d'Armide, Les Sylphides* (a revision of his earlier *Chopiniana*), and *Cléopâtre*, a reworking of *Une Nuit d'Egypte* first seen in St Petersburg. These, with a divertissement, *Le Festin*, and the operatic stagings, made up the repertory for the season. Its importance lay not only in the quality of the dancing and the choreography, but also in the distinction of the musical performances and in designs by Diaghilev's associates – Benois for *Pavillion* and *Les Sylphides*, Léon Bakst for the opulent *Cléopâtre*, and the essentially Russian Nikolay Rerikh for *Prince Igor*.

In this first season, which was no more than a brief visit by artists on leave from the Imperial Theatres, a pattern was set for the entire future of the Diaghilev enterprise. This pattern became clearer in the following year, when the huge success of the 1909 visit had naturally to be followed by another season. The same forces were recruited but an additional cachet was given by the creation of two ballets. In one of them, *The Firebird*, Igor Stravinsky's music announced an entirely fresh identity for dance music in the theatre. In the second, *Schéhérazade*, Léon Bakst's vibrant designs abolished once and for all the concept of polite realism in stage decoration.

The dancers once again triumphed – Nijinsky and Karsavina being especially adored – and the only relative shock in the season came with the failure of *Giselle*. At Benois' suggestion, the Russian dancers were to return this old French ballet, forgotten for half a century in Paris, to its native land. But even with Karsavina and Nijinsky, and Benois' designs, *Giselle* seemed old-fashioned to a Paris audience thirsting for more novelties, for the exotic. It was his costume as Albrecht in *Giselle* which precipitated the Nijinsky scandal in St Petersburg during the following winter and led to his dismissal from the Imperial Theatres. The Dowager Empress had found Nijinsky's costume shocking. Nijinsky refused to pay the fine imposed on him and was duly fired. Diaghilev, who loved him, had now the inevitable task of providing a framework for Nijinsky's genius. By engaging artists from the Imperial Theatres in both St Petersburg and

The Firebird was first staged by the Diaghilev ballet in 1910, and was handsomely redesigned in 1926 by Natalia Goncharova. This picture shows the production as revived for the Sadler's Wells Ballet by Serge Grigoriev and Lubov Tchernicheva in 1954. Svetlana Beriosova and Michael Somes are seen in the closing moments of the ballet.

Moscow, with Fokine as choreographer, Grigoriev as *régisseur* and Cecchetti as principal teacher, Diaghilev now formed a permanent Ballet Russe company.

For the company 1911 was to be a golden year. It toured extensively – this was to be its role thereafter – and in *Petrushka* was presented a perfect theatre work in which Stravinsky's music, Benois' designs and Fokine's choreography united with a unique singleness of aim. But by the following

Tamara Karsavina and Vaslav Nijinsky in *Le Spectre de la Rose*. Karsavina's beauty and the other-worldly quality that Nijinsky could assume are evident in this posed photograph.

season a further trait in Diaghilev's character had emerged. This was his incessant and restless quest for the new. It manifested itself in his wish to make Nijinsky a choreographer. Fokine was by now predictable as a choreographer and Diaghilev channelled some of his own creative energy into guiding Nijinsky.

The resultant creation was *L'Après-midi d'un faune*, given in Paris in May 1912. In it Nijinsky rejected the classical 'turn-out' and all the technical attitudes in which he had been educated. *Faune*, with its walking-step vocabulary and its two-dimensional frieze-like manner, is the first truly new choreography of the twentieth century in its attempt at re-creating an ancient Greek idyll. Superbly designed by Bakst, it yet caused a scandal because the faun's final gesture in sinking his body on to a nymph's veiling was thought to be obscene. For the rather prickly Fokine, Diaghilev's promotion of Nijinsky as a choreographer was enough to make him resign, and for the 1913 season Diaghilev had the 24-year-old Nijinsky as both principal dancer and sole choreographer. Nijinsky continued exploring entirely innovatory methods of choreography. His *Jeux*, with a score commissioned from Debussy, was a curious flirtation between a boy and two girls dressed for tennis and hinting at homosexual intrigue. His *Le Sacre du Printemps* was conceived in a primitive style of movement to match the pounding energies of Stravinsky's score. This evocation of ancient Russia (in designs by Nikolay Rerikh, an artist fascinated by Russian prehistory) assaulted both the ears and eyes of Paris, who howled their dislike of something so uncompromisingly modern. Although it received only seven performances it was acclaimed by discerning viewers in both Paris and London, and can be seen as a brave and very forward-looking attempt to expand the frontiers of movement.

In the summer of 1913 the Diaghilev troupe – but without Diaghilev – went to South America. On the voyage to Buenos Aires on board *SS Avon*, Vaslav Nijinsky succumbed to the charms of Romola de Pulsky, a Hungarian admirer, and on arrival in Buenos Aires they were married. Inevitably Diaghilev, deeply wounded, had Nijinsky fired on the company's return to Europe. He had also to cast around for a

Vaslav Nijinsky and four of the nymphs in his *L'Après-midi d'un faune* of 1912. The costumes for the nymphs, designed by Léon Bakst, are masterpieces of painted chiffon. In the poses of Nijinsky, as the faun, and his companions, we see his use of the flattened,

two-dimensional manner which is the basic premise of *Faune's*
choreography – a ballet in which walking was raised to an art form.
In recent years, the revivals of *Faune* have been much enhanced by
the restoration of Bakst's magnificent Attic hillside setting.

replacement, and he succeeded in luring back Mikhail Fokine as choreographer and dancer. But Fokine represented the past: Diaghilev's most significant action was to recruit a young Moscow dancer, Léonide Massine, in 1914, to dance the role of Joseph in the projected *Legend of Joseph* which Fokine was to choreograph to a Richard Strauss score.

By the late summer of this same year the Diaghilev troupe had dispersed – the outbreak of war had sent the majority of the dancers back to Russia. Only Diaghilev with Massine, who was now his protégé, and a few friends including Igor Stravinsky, remained in Europe. In Switzerland in the following year Diaghilev set about re-forming a company and preparing Léonide Massine for a choreographic career.

The wartime years of the Diaghilev ballet are extraordinary. Despite the most appalling difficulties and a constant shortage of funds, Diaghilev seems to have been inspired to make an entirely new start for his company. The link with Russia had been in part severed (Diaghilev was never to return) and in Massine he had a brilliantly intelligent and very young talent to shape. With the assistance of Mikhail Larionov, the Russian avant-garde painter, he began to supervise Massine's artistic education.

Some of the company's activities were dominated by the urgent need to make money and keep the dancers employed. Thus two tours were made to the United States – the only visits made there by the Diaghilev ballet. The impresario insisted that Vaslav Nijinsky should appear. For the second tour, Diaghilev remained in Europe, and under Nijinsky's artistic leadership the tour was disastrous. Nijinsky staged his final ballet, *Tyl Eulenspiegel,* in chaotic conditions, and on the subsequent journey to South America with the company his incipient madness became apparent.

Meantime in Europe Diaghilev and Massine, who had also stayed behind, were working on the shaping of Massine's talents. Massine's first ballets were made in 1916. By 1917 he had produced three works, including the Cubist *Parade* which had been devised by Jean Cocteau with Erik Satie as composer and Picasso as designer. We can see in this work, and in the light show *Fireworks,* with its Italian Futurist decorations,

Léonide Massine created *Le Tricorne* in 1919, with designs by Picasso and a score by Manuel de Falla. Massine had an electrifying stage personality, and danced the Miller for thirty years.

how Diaghilev was turning increasingly away from Russian collaborators to the European avant garde.

The darkest year for the Diaghilev troupe was 1918 (the memoirs of Lydia Sokolova, an Englishwoman who was a trusted and much loved artist with Diaghilev from 1913 onwards, give a vivid account of the straits to which the company was reduced). The company was rescued from imminent collapse by a contract to appear in music hall in London at the Coliseum, where it reopened on 5 September 1918. Much had to be done to re-establish the company, but London greeted

Ballet Russe

the Russian dancers ecstatically. Ever a loyal audience, London rejoiced in this reaffirmation of pre-war delights and the new ballets on which Massine had been working in Italy and Spain were to win every heart. These were *La Boutique Fantasque* and *Le Tricorne,* both premièred in London in 1919. But these must seem the last two great creations for some time. Touring was increasingly difficult in post-war Europe, and in 1921 Massine, following his marriage to the English dancer Vera Savina (Clark), split from Diaghilev. Finding himself without a choreographer, Diaghilev determined upon one of the most unusual decisions of his career – the presentation in London of a full-scale nineteenth-century classic. Inspired by the success of the musical *Chu Chin Chow,* which had played for over a thousand performances, Diaghilev thought that the opulent presentation of *The Sleeping Beauty* might give him financial stability during a very long run at the Alhambra Theatre, and also give him a breathing space in order to plan for the future.

Thus during the summer of 1921, backed by Sir Oswald Stoll, Diaghilev assembled *The Sleeping Princess,* as he called the ballet. He sought and found the finest components. For interpreters of Aurora he could call upon several great ballerinas who had fled Russia at the Revolution, and he further engaged his favourite dancer, Olga Spessivtseva, to come from Petrograd for the season. And, in a sentimental gesture characteristic of the man, as Arnold Haskell observed, he invited Carlotta Brianza, the original Aurora of the 1890 staging, to come out of retirement to dance her created role. Brianza needed too much time to prepare herself, which Diaghilev could not afford, hence she played the role of Carabosse. Another link with the original production was Maestro Cecchetti, who was teaching in London and who marked his fiftieth anniversary on stage by making a single appearance as Carabosse, his created role. The production was prepared by Nicholas Sergeyev (see footnote on p. 111).

To prepare a production in so short a time was a massive task. Diaghilev was helped by the fact that Léon Bakst, whom he had asked to design the production, had already produced the designs for a version which Anna Pavlova had staged and danced in New York in 1916 as part of a vaudeville

programme on Broadway. (Pavlova, after her vital contribution to the early Diaghilev seasons, had abandoned her
illustrious career in St Petersburg to become an apostle of the
classic ballet throughout the world. By 1912 her base for
operations was London, but from then until her death in 1931
she toured incessantly with her own company, dancing often
where no great ballerina had ever appeared before, and

**Ballet
Russe**

Anna Pavlova and
Mikhail Mordkin as
they appeared in
London at the Palace
Theatre in 1911. Both
were artists of strong
temperament, and
their relationship in
London was not
particularly serene –
at one performance
Pavlova slapped
Mordkin's face.

inspiring all who saw her. Her repertory was essentially light-weight but did include a number of classic stagings.)

Bakst re-worked his Pavlova designs to produce a production of surpassing beauty, probably unrivalled in grandeur and opulence in this century. Alas, Diaghilev this time had misjudged public taste. He had conditioned his audiences to expect constant novelty and the short-winded delights of the one-act ballet. The leisurely grandeur of *The Sleeping Princess*, and the academic refinement of the style, could not sustain public interest beyond 105 performances, and the ballet closed on 4 February 1922. Diaghilev was left with massive debts, an obligation to Stoll, and a company in worse condition than when he embarked upon the ballet.

The troupe set out upon another European tour – the last act from *The Sleeping Princess* was salvaged as *Aurora's Wedding,* and one other advantage emerged from the staging. Bronislava Nijinska, Nijinsky's sister, had been a member of the first seasons of the Russian Ballet. She had left when her brother was dismissed, but returned to dance in *The Sleeping Princess* and also to produce a couple of choreographic numbers to replace some Petipa items. Her talent was sufficient for Diaghilev to see in her a choreographic successor to Massine, and her first ballet, *Le Renard,* was given in May 1922. By the end of this year another major event in the history of the Ballet Russe took place. The company found a home. The Principality of Monaco offered Diaghilev and his dancers a contract to spend six months in residence, presenting ballets and dances in operas. Since the company also had two months' annual leave, this meant that Diaghilev had only to find touring dates for a further four months of the year, and the company's regular round of visits to London, Paris, Spain and Italy would easily fill these. For the first time an element of stability entered the gypsy life of the company.

Nijinska was to produce several important works in the next couple of years. Chief among these was her

Left: Olga Spessivtseva in the second act of *Giselle* in the 1930s. After dancing Aurora for Diaghilev she appeared variously in the West until her mental breakdown. She is considered by many to be the greatest classical dancer of the century.

The final scene of Bronislava Nijinska's *Les Noces*, as staged by her for the Royal Ballet at Covent Garden, with Svetlana Beriosova (standing) as the Bride. Nijinska succeeded in showing the very essence of Russian peasant faith with complete clarity.

monumental version of *Les Noces* in 1923 and the delicious frivolities of *Les Biches* in 1924. The company's residence in Monte Carlo inevitably brought an increased reliance upon French collaborators during the latter part of the 1920s. The twenty works produced between 1923 and 1929 were in the main more light-weight and more ephemeral than those from the pre-war years. Fashion was (nearly) all, but the collaborators still represented the cream of French taste: Marie Laurencin, Georges Braque, Picasso, Pedro Pruna, Maurice Utrillo, Max Ernst and Joan Miró, André Derain, André Bauchant, Giorgio de Chirico and Georges Rouault as designers; Erik Satie, Francis Poulenc, Georges Auric, Darius Milhaud, and Henri Sauguet among the composers.

There was a stress upon youth in much of the work of the company. Young dancers like Anton Dolin, Serge Lifar, and even the child Alicia Markova, who was asked to join the company when just fourteen years old; young designers and young composers, like Constant Lambert who at the age of twenty was commissioned to write the score for *Roméo et Juliette,* now dominated the Diaghilev entourage, which had gained in Boris Kochno, Diaghilev's secretary, a young poet who was to become very influential. A new young choreographer was also found. Bronislava Nijinska left Diaghilev following a quarrel; Léonide Massine returned to make occasional works; but the important new creative impulse came with the arrival of George Balanchine.

In the summer of 1924 a group of four young dancers had left Leningrad where they trained and were soloists with the State Ballet, to make a tour of the Baltic. They did not return to Russia; instead, making their way westward, they finally joined the Diaghilev company. They were Alexandra Danilova, Tamara Gevergeva, Nicholas Effimov and George Balanchine (Balanchivadze). Balanchine had already made his first choreographies in Russia. Diaghilev engaged him to produce opera-ballets for Monte Carlo and soon entrusted him with ballets. His first work for the company was *Barabau* in 1925, but it was in 1928 that Balanchine in a sense found himself when given Stravinsky's score for *Apollo* to stage. In its purity and classic economy we can see the future path that Balanchine was to take in the United States. For Diaghilev, this masterpiece and Balanchine's two ballets of the following year, *Le Bal* and *The Prodigal Son,* showed a magnificent upsurge of creativity.

The company was strong, the repertory magnificent, their base apparently secure. In the August of 1929 Diaghilev fell ill in Venice and died. With him died the Ballet Russe.

after Diaghilev

In the half-century since then, the entire ideal of classical ballet in Western Europe and the rest of the world acknowledges a debt to Diaghilev. But inevitably, the loss of the Diaghilev company meant that instead of a single glorious troupe which governed taste and seemed unassailably excellent, there now emerged more locally influential companies:

in Britain the Vic-Wells Ballet had started in 1931 and was eventually to grow into today's Royal Ballet; in Paris, Serge Lifar was to restore the faded glories of the Opéra ballet during the next quarter century; in the United States Lincoln Kirstein made it possible for George Balanchine to put down his roots in America and begin the work which was to culminate in today's New York City Ballet.

Nevertheless the Diaghilev Ballet Russe ideal was to persist for another three decades in various manifestations. By 1932 the crying need for a form of 'Russian Ballet' was answered by the emergence of a company initiated in Monte Carlo by the charming and civilised René Blum. He was soon joined by Colonel W. de Basil, a one-time Cossack army major, who provided business acumen and was eventually to become a disruptive force in the enterprise. Taking up the standard of Diaghilev, the Ballet Russe de Monte Carlo was launched with George Balanchine as choreographer, Serge Grigoriev as *régisseur* (to stage the Diaghilev revivals), many of Diaghilev's former dancers and eventually the newsworthy trio of baby ballerinas, Tatiana Riabouchinska, Irina Baronova and then Tamara Toumanova. These young girls, in their early teens, were prodigious dancers, trained in Paris by the émigrée Imperial ballerinas, and remarkable stage personalities.

Balanchine contributed a few exceptional ballets and then left, to be succeeded by Léonide Massine as principal choreographer. Massine was to become the dominant figure in choreography in Europe in the 1930s, thanks in no small part in his decision to choreograph a succession of symphonies, beginning with Tchaikovsky's Fifth, which became *Les Présages*, in 1933. His audacity caused a furore among music critics at the time but it brought tremendous publicity to the

Right: Alicia Markova and Serge Lifar, stars of Massine's company, in the second act of *Giselle*. In the summer of 1938, the Ballet Russe de Monte Carlo, led by Massine, was playing at the Theatre Royal, Drury Lane, in direct opposition to the de Basil Ballet Russe at Covent Garden, and ballet fans had an ecstatic time running from one theatre to the other during an evening to catch the best of both companies.

Ballet Russe, which knew extraordinary success. Arduous touring round Europe and America showed the company that there was a huge demand for the glamour of the Ballet Russe in this uneasy age. But the clash of personalities between Blum and de Basil and also Massine resulted in a series of splits and shifts of power. By the end of the 1930s Massine was identified with the Ballet Russe de Monte Carlo while de Basil was mastermind to the 'Original Ballet Russe'.

The war in Europe meant that both these companies were to go to the Americas – de Basil via Australia and South America; Massine to New York and to extensive touring of the United States where the company was now directed by Serge Denham, a Russian-American banker. (René Blum died in Auschwitz.) Both companies were victims of the power manipulations of the impresario S. Hurok, who presented them throughout the United States. The Denham company, led for many years by Alexandra Danilova and Frederic Franklin, lasted until 1962 and deserves credit for its popularisation of ballet throughout the United States.

De Basil brought his company back to Covent Garden in 1947 but the repertory was in tatters and the London audience found 'the Russian Ballet' a mere ghost of itself. Their affections and loyalties were now given to the national ballet – the Sadler's Wells Ballet – which had been installed the year before at Covent Garden.

the growth of ballet in Britain

Britain's national ballet had grown from the handful of dancers, led by Ninette de Valois, who had given their first performance as the Vic-Wells Ballet at the Old Vic Theatre in London on 5 May 1931. The company was based, thanks to Lilian Baylis – a woman of remarkable vision who managed the Old Vic and Sadler's Wells as homes for drama and the lyric theatre – at Sadler's Wells, which she had had rebuilt and reopened in 1931. Since 1926 Ninette de Valois had been working towards this event. She had laid the proper foundations: she had a school (which she moved into the theatre), a small repertory and she ensured the future of her troupe by guaranteeing contracts. Within four years of entering the Wells she had acquired the classical stagings which were to be another foundation of her company (all mounted by Nicholas Sergeyev* and made possible by the presence of Alicia Markova, a superlative classical ballerina then in her early twenties).

By 1939 the Vic-Wells Ballet was strong enough to present *The Sleeping Beauty* as the culminating achievement of eight years' work. Markova had left in 1935 to form the Markova–Dolin company, and was now a ballerina of the Ballet Russe de Monte Carlo. Her roles had been inherited by several young Vic-Wells dancers, one of whom was Margot Fonteyn. With the Australian-born dancer Robert Helpmann as her partner Fonteyn emerged as the company's ballerina in the late 1930s, and it was she who first sustained the *Beauty* staging as Princess Aurora, delighting the faithful audiences at Sadler's Wells, who had provided such valuable and dedicated support to the Vic-Wells Ballet.

Fonteyn had the inestimable advantage of growing up (she was only twenty when she danced Aurora) during the

---

* Nicholas Sergeyev (1876–1951) was born in St Petersburg, and on graduating from the Imperial Ballet School became a dancer and then *régisseur* charged with the proper stage-presentation of the ballet repertory at the Maryinsky Theatre in St Petersburg from 1904 to 1917. Following the Revolution of 1917, he quit Russia and came to the West, bringing with him the notation of the repertory of the Imperial Ballet in Stepanov script. From these priceless records and from his own exceptional knowledge of the old ballets he was to revive works – *Sleeping Beauty, Swan Lake, Coppélia, Giselle, The Nutcracker*, among others – for many companies, including Diaghilev's Ballet Russe, the Paris Opéra, the Vic-Wells Ballet, and International Ballet. It is from these stagings that Western ballet acquired the texts and understanding of the great nineteenth-century classics which have been and remain so vital in providing a basis for future development. It is a tragedy that much of Sergeyev's careful reconstruction of the old ballets has been jettisoned and probably lost through the wilfulness and insensitivity of later producers and ballet stars who chose to interpolate their own alterations and amendments – none superior to the originals – rather than respecting the basic texts which Sergeyev provided.

**the growth
of ballet
in Britain**

years when Markova was setting the classic example; Markova's departure, and hence the opportunities for young dancers to assume her roles, coincided with the arrival of Frederick Ashton as choreographer to the company. Moreover, from the beginning de Valois had, in Constant Lambert (1905–51), found not only a great conductor for ballet but a musical conscience and a guide of unquestioned artistic integrity and taste, as well as a most distinguished composer.

In Ashton the Vic-Wells (later the Sadler's Wells, later still the Royal) Ballet found the classic choreographer who was to help shape the English style of dancing during the next thirty years. Born in Lima, Peru, inspired by the performances of Anna Pavlova to become a dancer, Ashton fell under the formative influence of Marie Rambert when he came to London, where he eventually quit his office job to become a dancer. Marie Rambert had settled in London during the First World War and married the English playwright Ashley Dukes. She had first been impressed by Isadora Duncan in her native Warsaw. Subsequently she had studied eurhythmics (a system of musical training through bodily movement) with Emile Jaques-Dalcroze, and was engaged by Diaghilev to help Nijinsky elucidate the complexities of Stravinsky's score for *Le Sacre du Printemps.* By the early 1920s she had opened a school in London which was to become a cradle of British ballet. It was Rambert who urged several of her students along the paths of creativity. In addition to Ashton, she fostered the creative talents of Antony Tudor, Andrée Howard, Walter Gore, Frank Staff and many others – these were to be the makers of British ballet in the 1930s and 1940s.

Rambert presented a series of performances by students from her school, and from these came the Ballet Club presentations at the little Mercury Theatre which were the basis of the Ballet Rambert whose activities were an interesting creative parallel to those of the Vic-Wells Ballet. The Rambert company became associated with small-scale but distinguished ballets – described at the time as 'chamber ballet' – while the Vic-Wells was more clearly in pursuit of the larger-scale classical repertory.

The war years, contrary to expectation, were to see an enormous increase in the popularity of ballet, brought on by nation-wide touring. Despite all difficulties, both the Rambert and Sadler's Wells companies danced to a new and enthusiastic audience. At the war's end the Sadler's Wells Ballet, which had in effect become a national company, found a truly national home at the Royal Opera House, Covent Garden. Its history thereafter is the story of exceptional expansion on the sound basis that had been put down in the 1930s by de Valois, Ashton and Lambert, as the Royal Charter, granted in 1955, made clear. The school was expanded to encompass both a junior residential and a senior school. The classic nineteenth-century tradition was continued by Ashton's staging of the first full-length classic British ballets, *Cinderella, Sylvia, Ondine, La Fille mal gardeé, The Two Pigeons.* Ashton's heirs and successors – the South African John Cranko who came to London in 1946 and Kenneth MacMillan – further extended this manner in such long ballets as Cranko's *The Prince of the Pagodas* and MacMillan's chain of full-length works (*Romeo*

Monica Mason as the Chosen Maiden in Kenneth MacMillan's *The Rite of Spring*, as staged by the Royal Ballet in 1962. The designs by the Australian painter Sydney Nolan helped to dispel the traditional view of the work as an illustration of Russian pre-history.

Lynn Seymour and Anthony Dowell in Frederick Ashton's *A Month in the Country*, as staged by the Royal Ballet at Covent Garden in 1976.

and Juliet, Manon, Mayerling, etc.). The range of short ballets included native-produced works by Ashton, de Valois, Cranko and MacMillan to which were added some central masterpieces from the Diaghilev era and works by major choreographers like Balanchine, Robbins and Tudor. This repertory was sustained by generations of dancers who passed through the Royal Ballet School or who came from the one-time Dominions. Such dancers as Pamela May, Moira Shearer, Beryl Grey, Violetta Elvin (Prokhorova, a product of the Bolshoy but married to an Englishman during the war), Michael Somes, John Field, Alexis Rassine, Alexander Grant, and the next generation of ballerinas, led by Nadia Nerina and Svetlana Beriosova, with their partners David Blair and Donald MacLeary, who in turn were succeeded by Antoinette Sibley and Antony Dowell, Merle Park, Lynn Seymour, David Wall, Monica Mason, Doreen Wells and today's principal artists, are guardians of an exceptionally eclectic repertory.

An important extension of the Royal Ballet's work came with the move to Covent Garden in 1946, when Sadler's

Wells was not bereft of ballet. A second company was initiated, whose identity was more youthful and more experimental. It nurtured many talents, both interpretative and creative. In various incarnations under the directorship of Peggy van Praagh, John Field and Peter Wright this company has fulfilled an extensive touring schedule and also produced a great deal of new choreography. Its stars – Elaine Fifield, David Poole, Doreen Wells, David Wall, Margaret Barbieri, Marion Tait and Stephen Jefferies among them – won a devoted public not only in London but throughout the country.

The post-war years for the Ballet Rambert were more chequered. A hugely successful Australian tour during 1947–49 did much to popularise ballet in that country, but it depleted the Rambert coffers of both dancers and money. The need to tour in Britain inhibited the company's creative life. The need to provide a standard classical repertory, though skilfully met with excellent stagings of *Giselle* and later *La Sylphide,* stretched the resources of the company too far. By the mid-1960s the troupe was in dire straits. It was rescued by the decision to reorganise it as a 'contemporary' ensemble very much after the fashion of the experimental Nederlands Dans Theater.

Norman Morrice, whose decision this was, was to direct the company thereafter in a successful change of image. His own choreography, the ballets acquired from Glen Tetley and those produced by Christopher Bruce, a distinguished dancer with the troupe, all showed the Ballet Rambert to new advantage and to a new audience.

Rambert's new audience was also to prove the support for the most innovative development in dance in Britain – the emergence of a contemporary dance company in the late 1960s.

contemporary dance

By the time it reached Britain contemporary, or 'modern', dance was as old as the century. Its origins lie in the reaction against the sterile classic dance at that time manifest in the work of several pioneers. The first of these, Loïe Fuller 1862–

Above: Isadora Duncan in middle life when personal tragedy had so
clouded her art.

Right: Lynn Seymour dancing in *Five Brahms Waltzes in the Manner
of Isadora Duncan*, which Frederick Ashton created for her to dance
at the 50th anniversary gala of the Ballet Rambert in 1976. He based
the dances upon his own memories of Duncan.

contemporary dance

1928, was not a dancer in the accepted sense. Her performances consisted in the skilled manipulation of fabric in multi-coloured light. By this means she created images which were a form of sculpture, lacking in dynamics but immediately attractive to the eye. The true Earth Mother of modern dance is her fellow American Isadora Duncan (it is not insignificant that the new dance came from the New World). Born in San Francisco in 1878, Duncan came to Europe with her family. There she astounded the art world with a concept of dance entirely free. She was inspired by the movement she observed in nature and by the images she extracted from classic Greek art. Never a great technician, Duncan triumphed through a natural and compelling gift for movement and her charisma as a performer and as a woman. Her life, marked by scandals and tragedy, by improvidence and impetuosity, is celebrated in the massive testimony of artists and writers. But what Duncan did was to suggest a new freedom to inspire other practitioners. The most significant of these was Ruth St Denis. Born in New Jersey in 1877, St Denis made her first great successes in dances in exotic styles. She formed a partnership with Ted Shawn, and they toured America and the world with highly theatrical and very polished dance productions. To provide artists for their company they founded schools – both company and schools bore the name Denishawn – and from these there emerged the two most influential figures of American modern dance: Martha Graham and Doris Humphrey.

It is the work of these two women which was to provide the impetus for the great expansion of contemporary dance in America during the 1930s and 1940s. Graham is the pre-eminent figure by virtue of the fact that she set about the essential codification of the movement style – her classes, and the principles of 'contraction and release' which lie at the heart of her dance manner, were to be the grammar for much subsequent modern dance creativity. Doris Humphrey, with her fascination with matters of balance and the ideas of 'fall and recovery', was a parallel creative force in America. From the teaching of these two, and from their choreographies, have come all the attitudes which succeeding generations of Americans have accepted, adapted or rejected. But in every case their influence is central.

Appalachian Spring, with its Aaron Copland score, is one of Martha Graham's most famous works, dating from 1944. An example of her American period, it tells the story of frontier people setting up home in the West. The original cast is seen here with May O'Donnell as the Pioneering Woman, Martha Graham as the Bride and Erick Hawkins as the Bridegroom. The design is by the eminent Japanese-American sculptor, Isamu Noguchi, who has decorated many Graham works.

119

Even today Graham's company and the corpus of her choreography remain a vital point of reference for consideration of modern dance in America.

contemporary
dance

The development of American modern dance is a pattern of secessions precisely similar to the fact of Graham and Humphrey having left Denishawn. Such figures as Merce Cunningham, José Limón, Paul Taylor, and Twyla Tharp, and the 'post-modern' generation typified by Douglas Dunn, have repeated this amoeba-like splitting by moving on, or moving away from, a parent troupe in which they learned their craft. The present richness and diversity of contemporary dance in America reflects the vitality of the style and the constant questioning of attitudes which has ever been one of the strengths of the movement.

In Europe, the example of Isadora Duncan and Ruth St Denis was to be accepted in rather different terms through the emergence of what is conveniently called a Central European style of free dance. This is initially associated with the German Mary Wigman, and was furthered by many experimentalists during the 1920s and 1930s with the names of Kurt Jooss as choreographer and Rudolf von Laban as theorist being of particular relevance. (It is worth noting that the Wigman style was taken to America by Hanya Holm in the early 1930s and became part of the fabric of American modern dance.)

However, modern dance in Europe in the post-war years owes almost everything to the American example; a typical case being the founding of the London School of Contemporary Dance and its associated company which came about as a result of the decision to introduce serious Graham technique studies into Britain. The distinguished Graham dancer and teacher Robert Cohan was invited to London through the generous patronage of the dance lover Robin Howard, and within a decade an outstanding company of dancers and a fine school had emerged, with Howard and Cohan as guiding forces behind the enterprise, and a new

Left: Twyla Tharp and two members of her company in *Eight Jelly Rolls*. Her ability to turn the forms of popular dances into the most brilliant theatrical movement is one of the great gifts of this important figure in dance in America today.

121

generation of young British modern dance choreographers was being produced.

It is to these products of the London School of Contemporary Dance and the London Contemporary Dance Theatre that we owe so much of the developing interest in contemporary dance in Britain. Such dancers and choreographers as Richard Alston, Robert North, Ross McKim, Siobhan Davies, Micha Bergese are all products of the organisation and it is significant that in 1981 Robert North became director of Ballet Rambert, where Alston had the year before been appointed principal choreographer. Both have also had their works produced in companies abroad; other artists from this nursery of talent have been involved in the many small concert groups and solo recitals of contemporary dance which are now a feature of the British dance scene. The acceptance of dance – in all its many forms – as part of a wider cultural experience in Britain owes a great deal already to the tremendous initiative of Robin Howard and Robert Cohan in the 1970s. It is a matter for pride that the London Contemporary Dance Theatre has travelled throughout the world to great acclaim, even taking this British development of Graham Modern Dance back to the United States in triumph.

the spread of classical ballet

While America was discovering the importance of contemporary dance in the 1930s it was also to discover the importance of the classic academic dance. Ballet had been known in America since the latter years of the eighteenth century but the first serious attempt at implanting the style in the United States came with the invitation to George Balanchine to set up a school and company in 1933. The aim of Lincoln Kirstein, Balanchine's patron, supporter and director to his companies, was to encourage an authentically American classic ballet avoiding all the clichés and decoration associated with the Ballet Russe companies of the 1930s. There has resulted from this the New York City Ballet and the School of American Ballet, both glorious and dominant forces in the ballet of our century.

Siobhan Davies and Patrick Harding-Irmer of London Contemporary
Dance Theatre in Robert Cohan's *Forest*. Siobhan Davies, in addition
to being a fine dancer, is a gifted choreographer; Harding-Irmer is
one of the most outstanding dancers in Britain. This action shot
shows something of the energy and control of dancers trained in the
British contemporary style.

The New York City Ballet has always been a 'choreographers company', dedicated essentially to showing the
work of George Balanchine, greatest dance creator of our
time. It is resolutely unstellar, though filled with brilliant and
starry dancers. The only other comparable American troupe is
American Ballet Theatre. Founded in 1939 by Lucia Chase
and Richard Pleasant, it is the antithesis of New York City
Ballet. Eclectic in choreography, it has always been sustained
by its star dancers, who have numbered many of the greatest
artists in the world of ballet, from Markova and Dolin, Irina
Baronova, Nora Kaye, Alicia Alonso, Igor Youskevitch and
Erik Bruhn, to Natalia Makarova and Mikhail Baryshnikov
(who now directs the company).

A contributory factor to the emergence of a lively
regional activity in ballet throughout the United States has
been the prodigious expense of touring ballet. The larger
companies can now only play a few remunerative dates; the
days of interminable 'one-night stands' across America
(undertaken by the tours not only of the Ballet Russe companies and American Ballet Theatre, but also by the Sadler's
Wells Ballet in the 1950s) have ended. Thus companies have
been established to present classical ballet in many important
centres in the United States. Oldest of these is the San Francisco Ballet; in post-war years companies have been eagerly
supported in cities across America.

A comparable expansion of ballet can be observed
throughout the world. The example of the Royal Ballet
inspired the establishing of the National Ballet of Canada,
which is the largest of the Canadian companies: the other
major troupes are the Royal Winnipeg Ballet and Les Grands
Ballets Canadiens. Similarly, the emergence of the Australian
Ballet owes everything to the activities of Dame Peggy van
Praagh and Sir Robert Helpmann in shaping the company
after the image of the Royal Ballet, although its roots lay in the

Left: Merrill Ashley of the New York City Ballet in Balanchine's
Allegro Brillante. Merrill Ashley is a dazzling ballerina, endowed
with prodigious speed and superb clarity of line, as well as a sense of
joy in dancing.

company formed in Australia in the aftermath of Ballet Russe visits in the 1930s by Edouard Borovansky, himself a Ballet Russe dancer. The pattern repeats itself in South Africa where the Capab Ballet in Cape Town is now under the direction of David Poole, formerly of the Sadler's Wells Theatre Ballet; it is pre-eminent in that country.

In Europe a remarkable expansion in balletic activity took place in the post-war years. The Paris Opéra had been dominated by the work of Serge Lifar as director of ballet since 1931. He had brought that company to a peak of excellence through his own phenomenal presence as an artist and through his encouragement of great ballerinas – Spessivtseva, Darsonval, Chauviré, Vyroubova. There was of course to be a reaction against such an 'establishment', and the emergence in 1944 and 1945 of the brilliant Ballets des Champs Elysées, with its young choreographer Roland Petit, was a triumphant and youthful assertion of the elegance of French taste and the distinction of French stage decoration. From that time onwards Petit was to emerge as the dominant figure in French ballet, and for the past decade he has directed the Ballet National de Marseille.

The Opéra continues as a great national ensemble, sustained by a superb school; the policy of regionalism in France has led to several interesting and worth-while companies based on opera houses in major cities which, like the Ballet National de Marseille, are adventurous in choreography and design.

In Germany ballet was to receive exceptional impetus with the arrival of John Cranko to direct the Stuttgart Ballet in 1960. In pre-war years Germany had no strong tradition of classical ballet. In post-war years companies had been established in many opera houses, but it was Cranko's achievement in making ballet something important in its own right, rather than just a poor relation of the opera, which inspired other houses to emulate Stuttgart's seriousness. The Stuttgart Ballet became an internationally acclaimed ensemble; and in Hamburg John Neumeier has succeeded in raising the status of ballet to something like parity with the opera company.

An impressive contribution to the international scene has come from the Netherlands, where two companies in particular, the Dutch National Ballet and the Nederlands Dans Theater, have explored both the traditional and the contemporary style with commendable adventurousness and have put the Netherlands on the ballet map.

The other phenomenon of post-war ballet has been the success of the Ballet du XXe Siècle in Brussels under the leadership of Maurice Béjart. Dedicated to a cult of youth, of massive spectacle, and of fine dancing, Béjart's company has won an enormous public, especially in Europe.

In Scandinavia the Royal Danish Ballet has continued to this day under the shadow of Bournonville's genius. The company has throughout this century sought to develop its own choreographers and to propound an image of itself more up to date than that of its Bournonville inheritance, but it remains essentially a company dominated by its creative past.

Men of the corps de ballet of Nederlands Dans Theater in Jiři Kylian's *Soldiers' Mass*, first produced in Holland in 1980. Set to Martinu's *Field Mass*, the ballet shows a troupe of fighting men prey to the tensions and terrors of battle.

Karen Kain and Peter Schaufuss as the young lovers in the final, joyous act of Bournonville's *Napoli*. A product of the Royal Danish School, Schaufuss mounted this successful and intelligent version for the National Ballet of Canada.

Its dancers are among the most beautifully and generously gifted in the world. An important aspect of the Danish Ballet has been its export of prodigious male dancers. Erik Bruhn was the classic exemplar for many dancers in the 1950s and 1960s. As a professor, the Danish dancer Stanley Williams has given the New York City Ballet the beautiful gloss of Bournonville schooling. Peter Martins and Ib Anderson, stars of the Royal Danish Ballet, are also stars of the New York City Ballet. Peter Schaufuss has enjoyed international stardom and has also made exemplary Bournonville stagings for companies such as London Festival Ballet, the Ballet National de Marseille and the National Ballet of Canada. In the 1960s the dancing and ballets of Flemming Flindt, dancer and lately director of the Royal Danish Ballet, and the performances by the ballerina Toni Lander, were also very important to the success of several companies.

the spread of classical ballet

the Soviet Union

Ballet in Russia by the first decade of the twentieth century was in a parlous state. The cumbersome masterpieces of Petipa were outdated. The new Russian Ballet was in fact Diaghilev's Ballet Russe, which never performed in Russia. Its influence was entirely in the West. What brought the much needed revival of ballet in Russia was the 1917 Revolution which changed the entire order of Russian society. With the Revolution many of the leading dancers emigrated, and several of them were to become influential teachers, notably in Paris and the United States. For ballet in St Petersburg and Moscow, so intimately linked to the court, the future seemed dark. It was the efforts of Anatoly Lunacharsky, who was in effect Minister of Culture and a trusted aide of Lenin, which helped secure the continued existence of ballet, despite prolonged and determined attacks by trades union and party activists who sought to alter and democratise this Tsarist art. Lunacharsky believed that the Russian people, inheritors of the entire cultural history of the nation, were entitled to enjoy this fine achievement of the Russian spirit. Thus the 1920s saw a gradual acceptance of ballet as an art for the people. This inevitably brought a change in the form of the art, both in manner and in matter.

The manner of dancing found a logical development through the teaching of Agrippina Vaganova, one of the great pedagogues of this century. A one-time ballerina of the Maryinsky Theatre, she developed a teaching method and an image for the dancers in Leningrad which extended the old Imperial style, without deforming it, to provide a base upon which all teaching throughout the USSR was eventually to be placed. It is a bolder, more exultant style, but still recognisably a fruit of the old Imperial Ballet's manner.

**the
Soviet Union**

Although many of the nineteenth-century classics were preserved – though severely edited – and enjoyed by the new proletarian audience, it was imperative that an alternative to the princes and fairies of the old ballets be found. The one-act experiments so associated with Diaghilev were largely ignored in Russia. The form of the new full-length ballets was established with the success of *The Red Poppy* in 1927, which dealt with the crew of a Soviet ship calling at a Chinese port and offering support to the oppressed Chinese workers. Thereafter two veins of inspiration were to prove very rich for the succession of large Soviet ballets staged in the 1930s and 1940s. The first was stories of workers' struggle – *The Flames of Paris* (the French Revolution) and *Laurencia* (oppressed Spanish peasants). The second themes were taken from Russian and world literature – *The Fountain of Bakhchisaray* and *The Bronze Horseman* (Pushkin), *Romeo and Juliet* (Shakespeare).

By the 1930s and 1940s there had been a great expansion in balletic activity throughout the Soviet Union and today there are nearly forty companies in major cities of the Union. Although all based on a classic foundation, they naturally also reflect the regional identity of folk-dance forms.

Vaganova's teaching was to produce a prodigious new generation of dancers. The appearance of her pupil Marina Semyonova in 1925 proclaimed a new breed of Leningrad ballerinas. An artist of truly radiant power, Semyonova, and then Ulanova and Dudinskaya and an amazing catalogue of later ballerinas, announced artists who used their magnificent technical prowess with a profound sense of dedication to the new cause of Soviet ballet. The male dancer was no less life-asserting in the Soviet repertory. The heroic themes of the new ballets needed heroic dancing. This it received, and continues to do so in the prodigious performances of stars like Vladimir Vasiliev.

The St Petersburg supremacy in ballet in Tsarist times,

Right: Raissa Struchkova and Alexander Lapauri of the Bolshoy Ballet in the *Moskowsky Waltz*, a spectacular duet by Vassily Vainonen. The catch as catch can excitements of this pas de deux were typical of Soviet choreography in the 1950s, and very popular with audiences.

**the
Soviet Union**

when Moscow was the merchant capital, can be seen in certain terms to have persisted in the Leningrad Kirov school and company of today. It is this company which has provided many of the most influential Soviet choreographers – Lavrovsky, Grigorovitch – as well as the ballerinas who were transferred to Moscow in the 1930s and 1940s to strengthen that troupe when Moscow became the political capital of the USSR. The Moscow Bolshoy Ballet was developed into a troupe of block-busting size presenting block-busting ballets – *Spartacus* the supreme example. Its own artists, headed by the blazing Maya Plisetskaya and the quintessential Moscow couple Ekaterina Maximova and Vladimir Vasiliev, represent a style that is notable for its energies and its exultant advocacy of the Soviet view of mankind.

But even in the bastion of Soviet culture that is the Bolshoy Ballet, factions and disagreements have been observed, and the publication in 1981 of Vadim Gayevsky's book *Divertissement* (which contains a swingeing attack upon Grigorovich) highlighted the dissensions and uncertainties which surround the artistic future of even Moscow's ballet.

5

THE
ELEMENTS
OF
BALLET

Dancing can reveal all the mystery that music conceals.

Baudelaire

Whatever else a ballet may not have – and we have seen ballets without design, without music and without costumes – it must have dancers. Traditionally ballet was a combination of music, design and dance, but in the second half of our century, when so many of the arts have been questioned about the nature of their ingredients, the components of ballet have undergone many changes. The reliance upon music has been challenged – ballets are danced both to great symphonies and to recordings of squeaking doors – and the nature of design has moved from traditional painted scenery to a random assembly of objects. The constant has been the dancer, and no matter what experimental developments, the basic means of expression in ballet has been classic academic dance. Though this language may change it has certain fundamental rules,

Mikhail Baryshnikov and Natalia Makarova, dancing with American
Ballet Theatre, in the grand pas de deux from the third act of *The
Sleeping Beauty*. Their pose suggests the authority of their classic
style.

and these are what the dancer learns from the very first lesson.

They are rules that every child learns in dancing classes: attitudes about the 'turn-out' of the legs in rotation from the hip-joint, about the 'pulling-up' of the torso; a set vocabulary of steps – always known by their French terminology, a reminder of ballet's education in its earliest days in France; rules about posture, a whole corpus of physical wisdom that has developed across the four centuries that have seen today's ballet emerge from social dance and classroom labour.

Young children who attend perhaps only one lesson a week acquire a first understanding of the disciplines and the difficulties, and also the great rewards, of classical ballet training. They are rewards of properly trained muscles, of good posture, of ease of movement. A real ability and desire to dance may manifest itself in these early lessons, but in order to achieve a professional career as a ballet dancer it is necessary to train seriously and consistently in a proper vocational school from about the age of eleven. It is here that the young aspirant begins to understand the selfless discipline and hard work which is essential if a professional career as a dancer is to be achieved. This discipline will last for the entire length of a dancing career.

Every working day begins, for students and professionals alike, with class. No matter where in the world you enter a ballet school, by mid-morning the sound of a piano can be heard coming from a studio where dancers are stretching and sweating under the vigilant eye of a teacher. Class is essential. The human frame is awkward, not to say cussed, and the classic academic style does not come naturally to it. Hence it has to be prepared every day for the work which it is later going to be called upon to perform. Muscles have no memory, though they can be encouraged to fulfil certain functions, and it is the daily battle with the human frame which is the way a dancer 'wakes up' physically.

Classical ballet depends upon two essential actions of the body, which are the result of its long theatrical history. These are *turn-out* and *pull-up. Turn-out* is the revolving of the entire leg from the hip-socket to an angle which eventually will reach 90 degrees from the normal front-facing position of the foot. Thus, when a dancer stands in the first of the basic five positions, the feet are in a straight line with the heels together and the weight evenly distributed. The reason for turn-out is not only the greater mobility it achieves but also beauty of line in leg and foot, and a greater strength of movement. (The turn-out *must* come from the hip-joint and not from the knee or ankle since this weakens and injures these joints. It is only to be achieved by very careful professional teaching: there is no 'do it yourself' in ballet at all.)

Pull-up represents the vital need for a dancer to stand, and to look as if he or she is standing, as tall as possible. A straight back, a head reaching upwards away from the shoulders, convey a feeling of 'lift' throughout the body. Similarly, the upper trunk lifts upwards away from the hips and the stomach muscles are as taut as possible – this relating also to the dancer's need to breathe deeply to provide the essential supply of oxygen which is vital to proper muscular function.

The five postions of the feet are the five vowels of the dancer's alphabet. A development from the social dance of the seventeenth century, they were codified and established by the end of that century and provide the basis for every subsequent action that the dancer performs. Arm positions have also been regularised to provide a basic and harmonious series of attitudes. All these fundamentals prepare the dancer's body for the essential fact of its need to look beautiful and easy in action, no matter how difficult or extreme the demands made upon it by choreography.

In any ballet studio you will notice a wooden rail at waist height running round the walls with, usually, at least one wall of the studio covered in looking-glass. The barre, as this rail is called, is there to provide the dancer with an aid to balance and correct posture. The looking-glass is a point of reference to which the dancer will turn (though *not* all the time) to check physical stance. Class begins at the barre with the first slow bendings and stretchings which lubricate the

Right: Students at work in one of the studios at the Royal Ballet junior school at White Lodge, Richmond Park, Surrey.

muscles and prepare the body for the later hard work of class. After *pliés* – from the French verb *plier* – performed facing first in one direction and then in the other so that both sides of the body are equally trained (see Glossary), the progress of the class moves from more complicated exercises at the barre to the same exercises repeated and extended in the 'centre' when the dancers move away from the barre to the main area of the studio. In everything there must be a concern for the gradual, careful and scientific preparation of the body. Hence floors must be of wood, and ideally should be resilient. Hence, too, the dancers wear practical clothes which allow entire freedom of movement of their bodies, but also make sure that all the muscles are kept warm. (Professional dancers, at the beginning of a class, often look as if they are protecting themselves with the contents of a rag bag. As the class progresses and the muscles warm up and the sweat starts to flow, the protective garments are discarded and the basic leotards come into view.)

Class is given by the figure who is most crucial to a dancer's life, the teacher. Always an ex-dancer, it is the teacher who helps the dancer to discover the potential of the body and who will often give the body its stage identity. For the teacher is concerned both with training the body and developing the dancer's awareness of its capabilities. Great teachers are very few and far between.

The usual accompaniment to a ballet class is a piano, and a good pianist can also provide a certain stimulus to the constant and grinding repetitions of steps which are the basic facts of ballet training. Steps are repeated, and repeated, and repeated and combined into small *enchaînements* (linkings of steps) which provide different challenges to the dancers each day.

At the end of ninety minutes, which is the general rule for most ballet classes, the dancers' bodies have been tuned up for the steps of virtuosity which bring the class to a climax. The work of the rest of the day still looms ahead for the professional dancer. For the student in a good ballet school there now follow the many other classes which add up to the comprehensive dance training in various styles, as well as general education for those at a junior school

Class is very democratic. Every member of a company takes it and there is no differentiation in step or rank in the class between the great stars and the newest members of the corps de ballet. What will make the differences in the company itself are God-given gifts of physique – from beautiful feet to ideal proportions – as well as temperament, a willingness to work even harder to develop technique, and the priceless gift of being able to communicate with an audience. This last implies the power to establish an extraordinary contact with the public. Rudolf Nureyev, for example, has but to come and stand on stage and everyone is aware of his presence. To become a great dancer is the product, of course, of unceasing hard work, but it is even more the developing of a natural and innate gift by teachers and by choreographers.

Great dancers, like all great artists, are born, not made. It is worth stressing that dancing is not only a most difficult profession, but also one in which many may feel they are called but very few are chosen. The possession of rare physical qualities, from a small, well-placed head to a beautifully balanced torso and limbs, is the basic requirement to be employed even in the corps de ballet of a great company. To progress further up the hierarchy presupposes even rarer gifts of dedication, hard work and temperament. And luck. This last refers to the fortunate aspect of the planets so that the right choreographer and the right teacher for the right dancer all come together. Margot Fonteyn was certainly fortunate in having Ninette de Valois, Constant Lambert and Frederick Ashton to guide her to greatness. Five years earlier the extraordinary chances of coinciding with the birth of the Royal Ballet would not have been there. Similarly, the young British Ballet owes much of its classical foundation to the fortunate presence of the young Alicia Markova as a ballerina capable of dancing the great nineteenth-century classics when there was no other English dancer able to perform them.

The ballerina has traditionally been the pinnacle of the 'establishment' of a ballet company. Her identity as queen of the art dates from the emergence of the ballerina as goddess in the nineteenth century. We are not too extravagant in seeing Taglioni as the first modern ballerina: the qualities associated with her dancing, the lightness and grace and extreme technical prowess which helped her dominate the stage, are qualities we expect of dancers today, and even the physical image of the female dancer in floating gauzy skirt, poised on the tip of her toe, her hair neatly dressed, persists from Taglioni's time until today. One of Markova's exceptional attributes was a lightness and exquisite sense of Romantic style which made her seem Taglioni re-born. In Anton Dolin's re-creation of the *Pas de Quatre* it was Markova who made real all the adorable lithographs of Taglioni, when she appeared as Taglioni herself.

The Taglioni-Romantic image of the ballerina was to change later in the century to an image of the ballerina as virtuoso, with a repertoire of tricks made possible by the exceptional technique produced in the Milanese school of ballet which developed from Carlo Blasis' training system. The use of pointe work was restricted to the occassional pose on pointe for the generality of female dancers in the first half of the nineteenth century. Certain of the Romantic stars were able to work on pointe – it was Taglioni who revealed its artistic possibilities as an image of supernatural weightlessness and flight – but it was not until Italian shoemakers started to produce a strengthened shoe that the prodigies of virtuosity on toe associated with the Milanese ballerinas were possible.

In Imperial Russia in the 1860s and 1870s the corps de ballet rarely went on pointe and it was only the ballerinas who were called upon to dance in this style. The arrival of such a star as Pierina Legnani from Milan was an important goad to the dancers of the Maryinsky. It was Legnani who first showed the Russians mastery of 32 *fouettés* – a trick which she interpolated into several ballets and still remains her memorial in the third act of *Swan Lake* – but her prowess was soon challenged by M. F. Kshessinskaya, whose success in this trick occasioned 'cheers from St Petersburg to Moscow', as one commentator noted.

At the turn of the twentieth century the Russian ballerinas of St Petersburg had absorbed a diversity of technical influences and transmuted them into the homogeneous and very grand Petersburg style. Dancers produced from this school were to be the dominant figures for the next half-century. They were the first stars of the Diaghilev troupe, while one of them, Anna Pavlova, became synonymous with the word 'ballerina' for the twentieth century.

The feminine domination of the ballet stage in Milan, Paris and St Petersburg inevitably meant that the male dancer fell into disrepute and a subservient position. Only Bournonville in Copenhagen preserved man's dignity as a dancer and his equality of identity on the ballet stage. In Paris there developed a taste for pretty girls playing the hero's role – the first productions of *Coppélia* and *The Two Pigeons* are good examples. In Milan, despite an exceptional training which could produce such important figures as Enrico Cecchetti, a diminutive Italian-trained virtuoso who was eventually to become one of the greatest teachers in ballet history, men took a very secondary role in the extravaganzas which were so popular during the latter years of the nineteenth century at La Scala. In St Petersburg, at least, the traditions of male training were upheld in the school and also allowed a brief outing on stage in the male variations which were part of the grand Petipa stagings.

The prerequisite for the hero was nobility of manner and often the brief moment of brilliance would be entrusted to a younger dancer, while the partnering and dramatics of the role were fulfilled by the noble premier danseur. For example, Pavel Gerdt (1844–1917), the first prince in *The Sleeping Beauty* and the Petipa/Ivanov *Swan Lake,* was a middle-aged man, but his dignity was thought essential for princely roles. Significantly the greatest virtuoso demands on a male dancer in *Sleeping Beauty* were those asked of the prodigious Cecchetti as the Blue Bird – a role which still defeats nearly every male dancer.

That male dancing was an art still preserved in Russia is most clearly testified, as we have said, by the success of the Tartar hordes, led by Adolph Bolm, who roared over the stage of the Châtelet Theatre in Paris in May 1909 in the Polovtsian dances from *Prince Igor.* Their virility and strength astounded Paris. No less astounding was the work of Vaslav Nijinsky – the new Vestris – whose virtuosity was used by Fokine for entirely artistic ends. In this lies the great importance of the Diaghilev troupe. Not once did Paris or the rest of Europe thereafter see virtuosity as an end in itself. Ballet was reasserted as an art rather than as either a cheap sexual display or an excuse for refined gymnastics and circus tricks.

After the first Diaghilev season the male dancer once again could be considered an active and necessary ingredient in ballet, but it took almost another half century of social change to put the male dancer on the same pinnacle as the ballerina – thanks especially to Rudolf Nureyev and Mikhail Baryshnikov – and make dancing an acceptable career for a man to take up, without having to run the cheap jibes against 'sissy' dancing.

Central to the uncertainties which always attended dance as a career have been the economic deprivations which resulted from going on the stage. Until very recent times it was only the most successful performers who could count on making any adequate kind of living through professional dancing. Hence it was hardly a career which a man would enter if he envisaged marriage and a family. Futhermore, the tremendous physical demands of dancing have meant that by the age of forty, at the latest, a male dancer has had to consider an entire change in his career at the moment when his muscles have lost the resilience of twenty years before. In middle life, when many other men would assume that they were reaching the best years in their career, the dancer had to set about learning a new trade. For the female dancer the problem was, historically, less intense since matrimony was the hoped-for refuge when technical ability declined.

These problems are still there for today's dancers, but at least the financial rewards are more realistic than they once were, and the expansion in all forms of dancing means that there are many more opportunities as teachers for dancers who leave the stage.

For women the glamorous image of the ballerina is still potent, though anyone with a practical knowledge of the

Right: Alla Ossipienko and John Markovsky of the Leningrad Kirov Ballet rehearsing Grigorovich's *The Stone Flower* during the 1960s. The photograph suggests the acrobatic daring often to be found in Soviet choreography.

theatre will realise that the glamour is illusory: dancing is a life of toil and sweat. Nevertheless, for the general public ballet is still the art of the ballerina, and though managements may determinedly avoid the idea of star status great female dancers inevitably grip public attention and attract a devoted following. Artists as diverse as Alicia Markova, Margot Fonteyn, Galina Ulanova, Maya Plisetskaya, Svetlana Beriosova, Nadia Nerina, Antoinette Sibley, Lynn Seymour, Natalia Makarova and Suzanne Farrell, to name only a few, have all won audiences and the most ardent devotion from their public. They have inspired choreographers, sustained seasons, upheld the classical tradition or been the motive power behind ballet companies simply through the magic of their presence on stage.

We have seen how the arrival of Diaghilev's Ballet Russe in the West in 1909 re-asserted the virility of the male dancer, but the social respectability of the female dancer had to be established in this century too. The professional female dancers in the eighteenth and nineteenth centuries had been notorious for moral laxity. It is only in our present century that dancers have won the social acceptance due to any interpretative artist, moral dignity and a living wage.

It is not without significance that the great Danish ballet-master August Bournonville, with his solid bourgeois aspirations, strove to gain recognition for his Copenhagen dancers as decent and honourable members of society. It was the example of another Dane, Adeline Genée, which was to encourage the acceptance of ballet dancing in Edwardian London as a respectable and delightful art.

the choreographer

In recent years there has been a move both to teach and to encourage the art of choreography by seminars and workshops. The result has been a flood of new dances, most of which are perfectly terrible. Fortunately for the future of ballet, young talent does emerge but it is the rarest gift among the creative arts to have true choreographic ability. It is self-evident that many creative artists – painters, poets, composers, novelists, sculptors – can work by themselves in the isolation of a study or studio and hide their mistakes from the world, and can also be advised during the period in which they are learning their craft. The choreographer, on the other hand, needs bodies on which to work, and must take up the time of dancers to create his steps and then use a stage and involve an audience as well as designer and musicians before knowing precisely how his brainchild will develop, and whether indeed the world thinks he has any creative ability. We meet here the great problem for any choreographer. Until curtain-rise on the first night he cannot know ultimately whether his ballet is all that he hoped it would be – like a cook he only knows how good the dish is when it comes out of the oven on to the table.

The prerequisite for being a choreographer is to have been a dancer, for only the most serious professional training will really prepare one for a creative future by providing the necessary vocabulary of movement and expertise to use it. Moreover, a choreographer learns best how to construct a ballet by dancing in the works of good choreographers, for thus he perceives 'from the inside' how dances are put together, how dramatic scenes are shaped, even such basics as how a master gets his dancers on and off a stage.

It is this acquisition of craftmanship that is so important to a choreographer; it cannot be replaced by the kind of arbitrary experience so often manifest in the innumerable splinter groups which proliferate on the fringe of the professional dance world, as dancers desert from one small dance group in order to form their own troupe to explore their creative hopes and dreams. It is in the hard professional world of major ballet companies that we see the practicalities of the choreographic art. Though choreography is a matter of 'inspiration' it is also far more a matter of the mechanics of a company repertory, the need for a new work, the demands for a role for a particular artist, and the choreographer has to submit himself to these rules. With most choreographers in classical ballet, creativity – once the call has come for a ballet – will depend upon whether he needs to make a plotless or narrative work, his task within a company being to provide

the
choreographer

the essential flow of novelties which whet the dancers' appetites for work, and encourage the public to return time and again to the ballet.

If plotless, the choreographer will probably work from the inspiration of a score which he has already contemplated using and which has been, in a sense, germinating in his subconscious. If narrative, he will set about looking for a score which will adapt itself to the theme he has chosen. Or else he will have a score commissioned for him, but in this case there is the inevitable consideration of the time that a composer will take to prepare the score. Given the choice of the ballet's style, it is evident that the music must come first, for this is the foundation upon which the choreography will rest. With a narrative ballet the choreographer may be lucky enough to be able to dictate to his composer the timing of incidents, and the general shape of the score. This was the rule with the ballet scores of the nineteenth century, from *Giselle* to *The Sleeping Beauty*, and it obtained also in this century from Fokine's collaboration with Stravinsky on *The Firebird* and *Petrushka*, to the Stravinsky/Balanchine collaborations, up to Ashton's work with Hans Werner Henze on *Ondine* and Kenneth MacMillan's with Richard Rodney Bennett on *Isadora*.

In these terms it is possible to understand choreography as a thrilling physical extension of music. This is the case with Marius Petipa and Tchaikovsky in *The Sleeping Beauty*, where the dance images are inextricably linked with the music, and in our own time it is supremely true in the work of George Balanchine. In how many of Balanchine's ballets do we see the dance as a most beautiful illumination and realisation of the score! With minimal design and an entire absence of dramatics Balanchine could extract from a score – from Sousa to Webern – a movement essence which seems the perfect expression of the music in dance. Other choreographers can impose a dramatic argument upon their score which can be

Right: Robert Cohan (left) with members of London Contemporary Dance Theatre who are in the cast of his *Waterless Method of Swimming Instruction*.

**the
choreographer**

miraculously apt – we have but to think of the absolute rightness of Tudor's choice of the Chausson *Poème* for the dramatics of *Jardin aux Lilas* – or so closely wrought in collaboration with the composer that music is unthinkable without the dance, as we know from *Petrushka,* where you have but to hear the music to see the action in the mind's eye. (There are certain villains in the choreographic world who also spoil music!)

Once the music has been chosen, the choreographer has to face the morning when he also faces his cast for the first time. Choreography is entirely practical and the fiercely busy schedules of a ballet company do not allow for time to be wasted. Once a group of dancers are assembled in a rehearsal room work must go forward. As Balanchine has observed, 'In making ballets you cannot sit and wait for the Muse. Union time hardly allows it', and Ashton has also commented, 'You have to get down and do the job.'

Most choreographers come to rehearsal with no more than the outline idea of what they are going to do. Steps will be evolved upon the bodies of the dancers as they are present in the studio – what has been germinating has been the score or perhaps the dramatic argument that is to be followed. Very rare are the choreographers who come into a rehearsal room knowing what steps they are going to set; for most of them it is a matter of painstakingly showing dancers what they want as the score is played over, section by section, bar by bar, on the piano. Sometimes a dancer will be asked to move in a particular diagonal in a particular way and from this the choreographer will extract a movement idea which he will then develop.

In a sense, choreography is a collaborative process, since the dancers contribute bodies, which may inspire the choreographer to try and show them off in a particular way, or they may furnish the first priceless step that will trigger off choreographic invention. But it is craftsmanship which will sustain the enterprise, and sheer dogged persistence. At the end of a couple of hours work a couple of minutes of enduring choreography may have emerged – rarely more, often less. Each day the patchwork of the ballet is put together as the dances are assembled, and it may be that the choreographer

will work on different sections of a piece on successive days
because of the availability of only certain members of his cast. Sometimes, too, a ballet will be begun in the middle, or with a crucial *pas de deux* which will set its tone.

The choreographer has to follow the hours allotted to him in a company's rehearsal schedule and sheer practicality demands that he must use the materials, the bodies, he has at that moment in the best way he can. A celebrated example of this need to work is the creation of *Serenade* by George Balanchine in 1934. At that time he had just arrived in the United States and he initiated an evening ballet class in stage technique. To give his dancers experience he decided to create choreography to the Tchaikovsky *Serenade for Strings.*

'The class contained, the first night, seventeen girls and no boys. The problem was, how to arrange this odd number of girls so that they would look interesting. I placed them on diagonal lines and decided that the hands should move first to give the girls practice. This was how *Serenade* began. The next class contained only nine girls; the third, six. I choreographed to the music with the pupils I happened to have at a particular time. Boys began to attend the class and they were worked into the pattern. One day, when all the girls rushed off the floor area we were using as a stage, one of the girls fell and began to cry. I told the pianist to keep on playing and kept this bit in the dance. Another day one of the girls was late for class, so I left that in too. Later, when we staged *Serenade,* everything was revised. The girls who could not dance well were left out of the more difficult parts; I elaborated on the small accidental bits I had included in class and made the whole more dramatic, more theatrical, synchronizing it to the music with additional movement, but always using the little things that ordinarily might be over-looked.'

(From Balanchine's *Complete Stories of the Great Ballets.*)

The extreme practicality with which Balanchine works is absolutely typical of the way many choreographers approach their task. What experience teaches them is not only

**the
choreographer**

how to use the diverse material which is going to form part of their dance language, but also how to communicate to their cast with minimal delay the ideas which the score has inspired in them. It must be remembered that many a choreographer will have saturated himself in music he is to use before coming in to the studio. Ideas will be germinating that he must know how to bring to fruition when faced with his dancers.

the composer

A comparable example of craft is associated with the greatest ballet score ever written, that by Tchaikovsky for *The Sleeping Beauty*. After having agreed to compose music on the idea of *The Sleeping Beauty* in 1888, Tchaikovsky received from the choreographer Marius Petipa a detailed scenario which amounted to a break-down, act by act, scene by scene, dance by dance, of what he envisaged doing and the type of music which he wanted. Such meticulous planning was usual with Petipa and provided no real problems for the resident composers attached to the Imperial Russian Ballet, whose abilities included the skill to produce waltzes, marches and mazurkas to order. Tchaikovsky was the greatest Russian composer of the time and yet he was able and willing to comply with meticulous demands from Petipa. Here are the comments that Petipa provided for the first act entrance of Princess Aurora in *Beauty:*

> From 16 to 24 bars, which develops into another tempo. For Aurora's entrance – abruptly coquettish 3/4 time. 32 bars. Finish with 16 bars, 6/8 forte. Grand adagio, very animated (mosso). The contest of the Princes. Occasionally the music expresses ardour, then Aurora's coquetry and later – broad and very noble music for the finale. Allegro for the friends – 48 bars, finishing with a Polka tempo for the pages. Aurora's variation. Pizzicato for the violins, cellos and harps or finally flutes and violins. Coda. Vivace 2/4. 96 bars.

Coaching and the handing on of tradition is an essential part of
Soviet Ballet's policy. Young dancers are carefully prepared for the
greatest roles in the repertory and they will take to the stage armed
with the accumulated experience of their predecessors, in a chain of
performance which may stretch back to the opening night of some of
the most famous ballets in the repertory. Here, Galina Ulanova, great
ballerina of the Soviet Ballet, is coaching Maximova and Vasiliev of
the Bolshoy in *The Nutcracker*.

**the
composer**

From such extreme requirements Tchaikovsky produced some of the sublimest music ever written for the theatre. The full text of Petipa's notes, which include a complete break-down of the drama and full indications of characterisation as well as musical instructions, offers an amazing insight into the creative procedures of a choreographer and a composer. They should also be required reading for every company producing *The Sleeping Beauty.* Alas, no company now bothers to go back to sources and to 'do their homework' before rushing to present this masterpiece.

It is essential, in fact, that *Beauty* should be maintained in as pristine and original form as modern theatre practice will permit. It is in the structure of the ballet, as in the prodigality of choreographic invention, that we understand how great a genius Marius Petipa was, not only in devising sequences of choreography to show off his dancers and to reveal character but also in giving proper momentum to the action and in contrasting brilliant dances with scenes of expressive production. In the great art galleries throughout the world the cleaning of old masters has often rid them of a thick yellow varnish, which distorted colour, and over-painting which has been applied to satisfy prudish conventions of later generations. It is the duty of any producer working on *The Sleeping Beauty* to consider this masterpiece very seriously in the terms of its original music and choreography and to endeavour to bring these alive vividly for the audience today, while respecting the proportions of the original work, and also the conventions of the classic dance style.

Today, as in Petipa's time, major composers are prepared to work to the second-by-second timing that results from the planning for a major dramatic ballet. Both Hans Werner Henze for Ashton's *Ondine* and Richard Rodney Bennett for MacMillan's *Isadora* submitted themselves to the disciplines of writing to a minutage supplied by the choreographer, just as other great composers have written for the cinema under similar conditions of timing.

While the choreography is being created parallel activity will take place with the design and perhaps with the orchestration of a new score, since the composer will have provided the choreographer with a working piano draft of his music so that the choreographer may proceed while the composer is getting down to the lengthy task of orchestration. There is a problem here in that a piano reduction of a score denies both choreographer and dancers any feeling of orchestral tone and texture. There can result from this a real shock when finally the full score is played at the first orchestral rehearsals preceding production. In writing the score for Kenneth MacMillan's *Isadora* in 1981 Richard Rodney Bennett provided a two-piano version for the choreographer to use in rehearsal so that something richer in sound would help creator and artists.

the designer

The collaboration of the designer is very important from the earliest stages of preparing a ballet. It may be that the choreographer will have decided that his ballet is a plotless work entirely about movement. In this case he will probably ask for absolutely minimal design. This absence of decoration is a keynote of much of the work of the New York City Ballet, where dancers appear on stage frequently in the basic black and white uniform of the classroom – tights and a T-shirt for the men, leotards or the simplest of tunics for the girls. This appearance has evolved through Balanchine's wish to clear his dancing of any decorative frippery. (However, many New York City Ballet productions indulge in elaborate costumes and scenery when the nature of the ballet requires it – for example *Union Jack* with it authentic kilts, *Vienna Waltzes* with its white ball dresses, *Bugaku* with its Japanese costuming.)

There has been an increasing reliance among ballet companies on this basic dressing of dancers. It is an attitude dictated partly by the need for economy (costuming and design is extraordinarily expensive both in making and maintenance – sweat rots fabric) and partly through the availability today of man-made fibres which can be used in stretch fabrics as all-over body-tights to mould and flatter the dancers' bodies, and which can be simply and easily

decorated. In ballets as different as *Voluntaries* and *Elite Syncopations* we can see the enormous range of decoration that can be made on a basic leotard.

Design for the classical repertory of the nineteenth century is dictated of course by the fashion for dressing dancers at the time of the ballet's creation. It would be unwise to seek to re-dress Wilis or Sylphides in anything but Romantic tarlatans. Similarly the Petipa repertory and the twentieth-century ballets which owe allegiance to it demand that the female dancers wear tutus, which were themselves a shortening of the longer dress usual in the middle of the nineteenth century. It was the Milanese ballerinas like Virginia Zucchi who shortened these enveloping skirts to show the new virtuosity which they had mastered. (The pointe shoe, that development of the rise on to the toes which began in the early years of the nineteenth century, is now integral to the art of ballet.) It is the very nature of the Petipa classical style to display the danseuse's legs and feet with the maximum clarity and freedom – Aurora's attitude in the first act of *The Sleeping Beauty*, the line of Odette's arabesques in the second act of *Swan Lake*, must not be obscured – and the entire design of these ballets must allow the choreography to breathe and permit the brilliance of the dances to flash. Anything that distorts the shape of the dancer in classical works, from puffed sleeves for the girls to unnecessary and effeminate decoration on the men's costumes, does ballet the greatest disservice. For the male dancer – so discretely swathed in tunic and little knickerbockers over his tights in the nineteenth-century theatre – a much greater freedom in costuming has emerged, which today comprises a basic jerkin and tights for the princely heroes of the classics.

For design 'in its own right', that is, for ballets newly made with the choreographer working in close collaboration with the artist, the possibilities are limitless, but there are certain basic rules. Set design must establish a mood or a location

Left: Chenca Williams and Alain Dubreuil of the Sadler's Wells Royal Ballet in Kenneth MacMillan's ragtime romp, *Elite Syncopations*. Both the dancers and the musicians of the on-stage band wear costumes of exuberant fantasy designed by Ian Spurling.

155

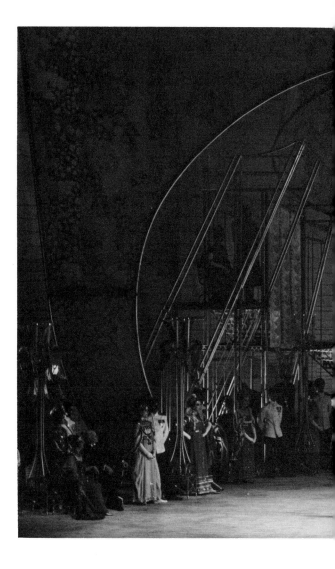

An outstanding example of British stage design is the décor provided by Barry Kay for Kenneth MacMillan's three-act ballet, *Anastasia*. The ballet tells the story of Anna Anderson who claims to be the Grand Duchess Anastasia, escaped from the Bolsheviks. Barry Kay produced a permanent setting which was used to show the Baltic sea coast, the interior of the Winter Palace (shown here) and a Berlin hospital.

in which the ballet moves, without overpowering the dancers or the choreography. The costumes must respect the choreography and must give the dancer and the choreographer complete freedom of movement. Anything which distorts the dancers' shape is bad; anything which impedes their movement has to be pared away. Sometimes, when costuming has to fulfil an historical function, it is necessary for both dancers and choreographer to work from the very first with a

simulation of the finished costume in order that movement
and characterisation shall be adapted to its requirements.
Thus a dancer will learn to rehearse with a cloak or a long
skirt or any other impedimenta of the finished costume.

In a ballet set in an historical period there comes the
very real problem of freeing the dancers' bodies to move while
yet respecting a period silhouette. Thus, for the three full-
length ballets by Kenneth MacMillan that he has decorated,

157

the
designer

Nicholas Georgiadis has had to convey the world of Renaissance Verona in *Romeo and Juliet*, the Paris of the early eighteenth century in *Manon*, and the Vienna of the late nineteenth century in *Mayerling*. It is some tribute to Georgiadis' great talent that he succeeded in presenting not merely a satisfactory solution to the sheer mechanics of period dress adjusted to dance terms, but also created designs which were imaginative aids to the dramas, transcending mere period reproduction to become works of art.

It was Diaghilev who first asserted the positive contribution to be made by the designer in ballet in modern times. His procedure was to choose the decorator whom he thought best suited to the ballet the choreographer had in mind. The result was an artistic marriage which owed not a little to Diaghilev's genius as catalyst and arbiter of taste. In the early years of the company his reliance upon Benois and Bakst was predictable since these two artists were friends and formative influences from his earliest years, but his turn towards European artists – Pablo Picasso for *Parade* in 1917, Henri Matisse for *Le Rossignol* in 1920, Marie Laurencin for *Les Biches* in 1924, and Georges Braque for *Les Facheux,* also in 1924, and Ernst and Miró for the surreal *Roméo et Juliette* of 1926 – suggests his uncanny ability to select the right painter for the new work which he envisaged. This list of painters suggests also the astounding quality of decoration in the latter years of the Ballet Russe. Such autocracy no longer exists; it is usually the choreographer who now chooses his designer and though this can produce very remarkable collaborations – such as the more than twenty years during which MacMillan and Georgiadis have worked together – it may also result in dull design, since not all choreographers have either good visual taste or much experience of the world of the painter.

One of the changes in stage design has been the move away from painted scenery to permanently built sets, which are adapted for a diversity of scenes in a ballet, or the use of metallic structures and atmospheric lighting. With modern developments in technology it is possible to light ballets with increasing subtlety and dramatic effect – London Contemporary Dance Theatre prides itself justifiably upon excellence of lighting, and it is the modern dance world which has best understood and made use of the possibility of light.

The American choreographer and man of the theatre Alwin Nikolais has created and entire genre of spectacle from projections, lighting and the use of properties. He is a magician of the theatre in that he alters the shape of dancers entirely by encasing them in stretch fabric or by shrouding them in vast draperies on to which he casts eye-deceiving patterns and forms. Nothing is ever what it seems in a Nikolais work. Though his choreography may sometimes seem minimal, the eye is constantly ravished by the spectacular effects of light and colour he achieves.

Alwin Nikolais devises the sound accompaniment, lighting and costumes with which he transforms his dancers into a variety of magical shapes. Here, the dancers are encased in stretch jersey sacks.

159

the
designer

The specialist stage designer as collaborator has brought technical assurance to ballet decoration; but he has also limited the range of decorative ideas. Where once balletic collaboration might involve an easel painter whose view of the stage was that of a canvas which he might fill with the richness of his imagination as an extension of the ballet's theme – an idea which was carried to excess when Salvador Dali designed some ballets for Léonide Massine in the 1940s – the specialist stage designer is much more a craftsman called upon to realise either a simple functional set or a literal recreation of an historical period.

A notable exception among choreographers of today is Roland Petit who has an eye for decoration and a willingness to engage the major artists of our time. Every Petit ballet provides some kind of positive visual statement. He has ranged from Delfau and Max Ernst to Christian Dior and Erté, a catholicity of taste which owes something to his early mentors, Christian Bérard, the most important French designer of the 1930s and 1940s who worked both in theatre and in fashion with a sublime simplicity, and Boris Kochno who was Diaghilev's secretary and also provided librettos and considerable artistic collaboration to the last years of the Ballet Russe.

on stage

It has been very justly observed that choreographers conduct their education in public. There is no way a ballet can be hidden, no way the choreographer, unlike any other creative artist, can hide what he has done, because it is not until it gets on to the stage that anyone can really tell what a ballet is like. It is only at the final dress rehearsal that all the components are brought together and can be assessed as a whole. No

Right: Bryony Brind and Michael Batchelor of the Royal Ballet in Jennifer Jackson's *Go and Touch*, made for an evening of new choreography staged to celebrate the 50th anniversary of the Royal Ballet.

amount of experience can tell anyone, let alone a choreographer, exactly how the ballet is going to look. Sometimes the choreographer does not understand the full implications of what he has done until the ballet has been run in through several performances. There is a real tragedy for choreographers that at the dress rehearsal there is no further time to alter, cut or expand the ballet that will be seen on the following night. Unlike musicals or plays, which may often have two weeks of previews in which alterations can be made and the cast can accustom themselves to the work they are performing, ballets are put on 'cold'. Thus, for a long new work – such as the three-act ballets by MacMillan and Neumeier – the first night is a make or break occasion, when the ballet itself takes the stage in what is a state of reasonable unpreparedness. Furthermore, critics and public are called upon to make an instant reaction, and the critics are expected to pass instant judgment – within anything from half an hour of curtain fall – which will stand as an immediate and permanent assessment of perhaps a year's work by choreographer, composer and designer. There is nothing wrong with immediate reaction to a work of art – most critics believe that they can tell within a couple of minutes if Baron Frankenstein has been at work in a ballet studio – but the nature of much day-to-day journalism requires snap judgments and sometimes superficial expression, and the resultant 'criticism' is far from valid or worthy of the term criticism. The demands of daily newspapers for an instant comment on a much publicised new work have to be met, but any critic worth his or her salt will return with an open mind for further viewings.

The ballet public tends to read the critics with whose tastes it has something in common, but ultimately the public makes up its own mind; it is only if the very large number of writers on dance in Britain, for example, come out unanimously for or against a work that they can affect the box office. And not always then – which is entirely as it should be.

Problems for the choreographer emerge if he wishes to edit the ballet he has made. These have to do with the shortage of time available for extra rehearsals after a work has been put into the repertory, and also with such problems as whether the composer will allow cuts in his score, or whether

an existing score will allow the excision of passages which suit
the changes to be made in the dance. For, with a repertory
company, there is the constant need to prepare new programmes, new works and new interpreters while maintaining
the standards of the existing repertory and dancers.

    Nevertheless, whatever the birth traumas which
attend the first performance of a ballet, works do find their
own level. This may take a certain time for the preservation of
good ballets which do not make an immediate appeal to the
public. If a company has faith in a 'difficult' new work that
does not have immediate audience appeal, it can nurse it by
placing it judiciously in a programme with popular works. It
then starts to worm its way into the hearts of the public – that
was the case with Ashton's *Scènes de Ballet* and MacMillan's
Song of the Earth in the Royal repertory, which have at last
been acknowledged as major works. Conversely, the real
stinkers in the repertory usually sink quite quickly from public
view and are only recalled when ballet-goers remember with
morbid delight especially awful evenings they have endured:
prime examples were Massine's *Le Bal des voleurs,* which
seemed totally confusing from start to finish, and Lifar's *Bona-
parte à Nice* in which the young Napoleon had a very difficult
time with members of the corps de ballet as a cavalry
squadron. The fact that these two misfortunes were by most
distinguished figures in twentieth-century ballet indicates
that the lightning of disaster can strike anywhere. Balanchine,
Ashton, Tudor, MacMillan, Cranko have all produced works
over which veils of silence have to be drawn.

    The failure of ballets by established masters of
choreography is an inevitable result of the fact of being a
craftsman, producing work to order. Though the layman may
speak of great choreographers as 'geniuses', the choreographer more often speaks of himself as a journeyman labourer.
(Balanchine described himself variously as a cabinet-maker or
a cook.)

But, ultimately, all the labours by choreographers, composers,
designers and dancers are the subjects of public taste. Our
aim in this book has been to stimulate an interest. We cannot

*on
stage*

influence anyone's reaction to any ballet – we know this from our experience as critics. We can, however, hope to communicate our own enthusiasm for the art of dancing and perhaps encourage an understanding of what ballet and dance offer to those who are prepared to go out and see for themselves. Some years ago the ballerina Alexandra Balashova, who made her début in the Imperial Russian Ballet in 1905, inscribed a photograph for us with the phrase 'The theatre is a temple in which I worship every day'. It is this seriousness and dedication to art which is the essence of the dancer's calling, that we, as an audience, have to respect and perhaps try to emulate.

Ballet is entertainment but it is also an art, and we must bring to it that respect which we owe to the creators and interpretative artists who have made the ballet live. To do anything less than this is to minimise ballet's achievements and reduce its power to move and delight us.

6

STORIES
OF
POPULAR
BALLETS

L'Après-midi d'un faune

Choreography by Vaslav Nijinsky, decor and costumes by
Léon Bakst, music by Claude Debussy. First produced by the
Diaghilev Ballet in Paris in 1912, this was Nijinsky's first
ballet.

A faun basks on a hillside in the afternoon sun. He sees some
nymphs going to bathe. Stirred by desire he descends from his
rock but the nymphs flee. One remains but then runs away,
dropping her scarf. The faun picks it up and returning to his
rock sinks his body on to the scarf as if it were the numph.

The first 'scandalous' ballet, *Faune* is more interesting and
beautiful than its reputation suggests. It is the first modern
ballet of the century, its movement based on walking steps
with the body held in an artificially flattened, frieze-like
position.

Afternoon of a Faun

Choreography by Jerome Robbins, music by Debussy. First performed by the New York City Ballet in 1953.

Afternoon of a Faun uses the same Debussy score as Nijinsky's *L'Après-midi d'un faune* but re-works the incident in modern terms. In a dance studio a boy ballet student sleeps, then starts to exercise. A girl student enters. Neither looks at the other but they gaze, as dancers do, at their reflections in the mirror – which is in fact the audience which forms the fourth wall of the stage. As they work the boy kisses the girl impulsively. The mood is shattered, the girl leaves, and the boy stretches lazily on the floor.

La Bayadère

Choreography by Marius Petipa, music by Ludwig Minkus. First produced at the Bolshoy Theatre, St Petersburg, in 1877.

La Bayadère is one of Petipa's greatest dramatic works and has been preserved by the ballet in Leningrad/Petersburg as a superb example of the nineteenth-century grand spectacular ballet. The action is set in India and relates how a young warrior, Solor, loves a temple dancer, Nikiya. She is also loved by the chief Brahmin of the temple at which she is one of the sacred dancers (bayadères). Nikiya rejects the Brahmin and swears eternal love with Solor over the flames of the sacred fire. But Solor is summoned by the local Rajah to be betrothed to Gamsatti, the Rajah's daughter. Gamsatti falls in love with Solor and Solor is strongly attracted to her. Gamsatti learns of his earlier love for Nikiya and confronts Nikiya with this fact – pointing out that a mere temple dancer can offer nothing in comparison with the wealth and power of a Prince's daughter. The agonised Nikiya tries to stab Gamsatti, then flees in horror at her own action – while Gamsatti vows vengeance.

In the second act, Solor and Gamsatti are betrothed and Nikiya is called upon to dance for them. As she does so she is presented with a basket of flowers in which Gamsatti has had a poisonous snake hidden. The snake bites Nikiya. She rejects the antidote offered her by the chief Brahmin if she will be his, preferring to die rather than live without Solor.

Solor is aghast at events, and to soothe his anguish smokes opium. In the dream that ensues he imagines himself in the Kingdom of Shades where he sees a procession of ghostly bayadères among whom he finds Nikiya. This Kingdom of Shades sequence is a masterpiece of pure dance, and one of Petipa's finest achievements. Solor dances with Nikiya.

In the final act, Gamsatti and Solor are to be married but the ghost of Nikiya appears to Solor and before the couple can be married the anger of the gods at the murder of Nikiya causes a great storm which destroys the temple and everyone within it.

In an apotheosis, Nikiya and Solor are seen united in a kingdom beyond death.

Although it has been much edited and altered in Russia, *La Bayadère* is honoured there as a masterpiece of nineteenth-century ballet. In the West, the Kingdom of Shades scene was shown by the Leningrad Kirov Ballet in London in 1961 and created a sensation by its beauty. It was revived for the Royal Ballet by Rudolf Nureyev, and in America Natalia Makarova mounted it for American Ballet Theatre, later following this scene with a complete production in which she edited and re-shaped the ballet to make a strong and convincing dramatic production.

Coppélia

First produced at the Paris Opéra in May 1870, with choreography by Arthur Saint Léon and with irresistible music by Léo Delibes, *Coppélia* is inspired by a story by the German Romantic writer E. T. A. Hoffmann.

Its first act tells of Swanilda, a pretty Galician girl, who loves Franz. Franz is a lad with a roving eye and he has been attracted by a beautiful creature who appears seated on the balcony of the house of Dr Coppélius, a mysterious old alchemist. Swanilda and Franz are supposed to be betrothed amid all the joyous dances of their companions but Franz is still paying court to the girl on the balcony and Swanilda is, justifiably, annoyed. Dr Coppélius appears on the way to the local inn after all the merrymakers have departed and, after being teased by some youths, he drops the key to his house. Swanilda and her girl friends find it and decide to explore his house and discover the identity of the mysterious girl. As the act ends, Coppélius returns seeking his door key, and finds his front door open: he enters in search of marauders. As the curtain falls Franz enters with a ladder, determined to climb up and discover the fair occupant of the balcony.

Act II takes place inside Coppélius's workroom. Swanilda and her friends creep in amid the gloom and are astonished to discover that Coppélius manufactures life-like and life-size automata. They set them in motion and further discover that the mysterious girl is also a doll, Coppélia. Coppélius enters and drives them out – save Swanilda, who takes refuge in Coppélia's little alcove. Franz enters through the window and is caught by Coppélius, who is amused to learn of his infatuation for Coppélia. He gives Franz drugged wine and prepares to make the ultimate experiment: the transfer of life into the doll Coppélia. He wheels in the doll from the alcove without realising that Swanilda has taken the doll's place and wears her costume.

Swanilda realises what Coppélius is trying to do and decides to trick him. To Coppélius' amazed delight his spells and incantations seem to work and the supposed Coppélia comes to life, boisterously mocking him, playing with the other toys and trying to awaken the drugged Franz. The scene is vividly comic and Coppélius makes Swanilda perform two brilliant solos before she succeeds in awakening Franz. They mock the old man and flee his work-room as he mourns in despair over the entirely lifeless body of the doll, Coppélia.

In Act III Franz and Swanilda are happily united and their betrothal is celebrated amid general festivities that mark the placing of a new bell in the little town. Coppélius is given money to compensate him for the damage to his workshop and his pride, and the ballet ends in a general burst of exuberance.

Sustained by its delicious score, *Coppélia* in various productions – most of them stemming from the version first mounted in St Petersburg in 1884 – has conquered audiences throughout the world. Originally the role of Franz was danced by a girl and that tradition lasted in Paris until after the Second World War, but elsewhere it has always been taken by a man.

La Fille mal gardée

Music by Ferdinand Hérold, with design by Osbert Lancaster and the score edited and arranged by John Lanchbery, originally staged in 1789, the charm of this ballet's plot guaranteed it a continuing existence throughout the nineteenth century, particularly in Russia. The ballet was given new life in 1960 when Frederick Ashton made his own version for the Royal Ballet.

In Act I, Scene I, we are in Widow Simone's farmyard. Her daughter Lise is in love with Colas, a young farmer, but Simone intends that she shall marry Alain, the witless son of Thomas, a wealthy vineyard-owner. Lise and Colas declare their love but Colas is sent packing and Thomas brings Alain to court Lise before they all move to the cornfield to celebrate the end of the harvest. In the second scene, at the cornfield, Alain tries to dance with Lise but Colas gets rid of him and the lovers dance an ecstatic and brilliant *pas de deux*. Simone is angry but is mollified when asked to display her skill in a Clog Dance. After a maypole dance a storm scatters the merrymakers.

The second act takes place inside Simone's farmhouse to which Lise and her mother return soaked by the storm. They try to get warm and when Simone falls asleep Lise attempts to escape to see Colas. Her mother thwarts her. Harvesters bring

169

in the stooks of corn to dry and Simone leaves the house,
locking Lise firmly inside. Lise dreams of marriage and
children and is amazed when Colas springs from among the
stooks of corn where he has hidden. The lovers are happy but
suddenly see Simone returning. Lise has to hide Colas in her
bedroom, but she is soon packed off there herself by her
mother to get ready for her betrothal to Alain.

The farmworkers watch as Alain and his father arrive and the
marriage contract is signed. Alain is given the key to Lise's
bedroom and when he opens the door he discloses Lise and
Colas in each other's arms. General consternation is
eventually followed by Simone's acceptance of the fact that
Lise and Colas must marry. The ballet ends with celebrations
– and a surprise.

The Firebird

The Firebird was the first score made by Igor Stravinsky for
the ballet – the commission came from Diaghilev who, with
Fokine the choreographer, was preparing a Russian fairy-tale
ballet for the second Paris season of ballet and opera in 1910.
Scenery and costumes were by Golovin (the Firebird's and
Tsarevitch's costumes by Bakst).

The action is a combination of several legends: the young
Tsarevich Ivan wanders into a mysterious forest and, climbing
a wall, finds himself in a garden where he sees a strange light.
It proves to be the magical Firebird, whom he captures. After
struggling to get away, the bird obtains her release by giving
Ivan one of her gleaming feathers with the assurance that
should he be in trouble she will come to his aid if he waves it.
She flies away and Ivan suddenly sees a group of young
women who enter the garden and play with golden apples
from a magic tree. Ivan approaches them and falls in love with
their leader, the beautiful Tsarevna, who warns him that he is
in the domain of the evil Kastchey. Sudden noises alarm the
maidens; they flee, and as Ivan tries to leave the garden a

magic wall comes down and he is trapped. Kastchey's horde of monsters, and prisoners of his enchantments, appear. Finally the magician himself enters, a horrible being who tries to cast a spell upon Ivan.

As Ivan faints he remembers the Firebird's promise. He waves the feather, the Firebird appears and immediately forces Kastchey's hordes to dance until they drop with exhaustion, at which moment the Firebird dances a lullaby and all sleep. The Firebird then tells Ivan to fetch a casket from Kastchey's domain. It contains an egg which is his soul. Ivan does so and the aghast Kastchey watches as Ivan throws the egg into the air and then lets it crash in pieces to the ground.

Darkness falls, and when the light returns Kastchey's enchantments are over. His prisoners have been restored to their human form as knights, who are betrothed to the beautiful Tsarevna's attendants, and Ivan and the Tsarevna are crowned as rulers of Russia: a final pose shows Ivan raising his sceptre in a noble gesture amid all the trappings of the Holy Russia of the Tsars.

Giselle

Choreographed by Jean Coralli at the Paris Opéra in 1841, with music by Adolphe Adam and designs by Ciceri, *Giselle* was a vehicle to star Carlotta Grisi; her teacher, lover and artistic guide, Jules Perrot, provided the choreography for all Giselle's dances.

The story is set in the mediaeval Rhineland where Giselle, a simple peasant girl, is loved by and loves a mysterious young man whom she knows as Loys. She is also loved by Hilarion, a game-keeper. Hilarion discovers that Loys is a nobleman in disguise and he decides to be revenged. He seizes his chance when a court hunting party, led by the Duke of Courland and his daughter Bathilde, arrives and asks for rest and refreshment at Giselle's cottage. Loys is then revealed as Duke Albrecht, betrothed to Bathilde. The shock of this news unseats Giselle's reason: she goes mad, dances in her madness and finally dies at Albrecht/Loys' feet.

Act II is set in a dim forest glade. It is nearly midnight and Hilarion has come to pray at Giselle's grave. He is driven from the place as midnight sounds and the Queen of the Wilis emerges from the ground and summons her subjects. These are Wilis, the ghosts of young girls, dead before their wedding day and over-fond of dancing, who arise from their graves as midnight sounds and dance any man whom they chance upon to his death. Giselle is summoned from her grave and initiated in to their rites. As the Wilis melt into the night, Albrecht enters, bringing flowers to Giselle's grave. Giselle appears to him, her love for him having survived the grave and he rushes after her into the forest. Suddenly the Wilis appear, hounding Hilarion to his death, and when he has been driven to drown in the nearby lake the Wilis discover Albrecht. Myrtha, their Queen, condemns him to dance until he dies. But Giselle urges him to seek the protection of the cross on her grave. Appeals for mercy are ignored and, though Myrtha cannot overcome the power of the cross, she forces Giselle to dance, which she does so beguilingly that Albrecht has to join her and his fate seems sealed. He dances, and as the night wears on Giselle tries to dance with him and sustain him. His death from exhaustion seems imminent but at this moment the first rays of the sun tell of dawn's approach. The Wilis must return to their graves and Giselle drifts away for ever, having saved Albrecht. He is left sorrowing and alone.

Isadora

Choreography by Kenneth MacMillan, music by Richard Rodney Bennett, design by Barry Kay.

The tragic career of Isadora Duncan is also a glorious affirmation of the power of one extraordinary talent to arouse fervent interest in a new form of dance. In 1981 Kenneth MacMillan choreographed a two-act fantasy abut the life and loves of Duncan which charted her story from her arrival in

London at the turn of the century to her death in Nice in 1927. Interwoven with dances evocative of Duncan's own manner are scenes which show her sexual conquests and the tragedies of her life, which encompassed the death of her two children and the tragic failure of every relationship – not least with the one man she married, the Russian poet Esenin. The ballet is a combination of dance and a dramatic manner which owes something to the theatre: the role of Isadora is taken by a dancer and by an actress who speaks Duncan's own words and at one moment dances the *Marseillaise,* one of Duncan's most celebrated numbers.

Konservatoriet

In 1849 Bournonville made *Konservatoriet* (or *A proposal by advertising*) as a two-act ballet, set in the Paris of the 1820s which he knew as a student.

The first scene was the re-creation of a class given by Auguste Vestris and, though the rest of the ballet fell from the repertory fifty years ago, this first scene has been preserved as a loving evocation of the style and manner of dancing which lies at the basis of the Royal Danish Ballet's achievement. It comprises a sequence of class-room exercises and *enchaînements,* given vivid theatrical life and making tremendous demands upon its cast, from children in the ballet school to virtuoso dancers in the company.

Manon

The Abbé Prévost's novel is a portrait of French society at its most corrupt in the eighteenth century. Kenneth MacMillan's ballet, first produced in 1974, uses music by Massenet – though none from Massenet's opera of the same name. The scenery and costumes were designed by Nicholas Georgiadis.

The story is of the innocent young Manon, on her way to a

convent, who comes to Paris to see her brother Lescaut, a thoroughly vicious opportunist. Lescaut is eager to sell Manon to the highest bidder but she meets a young seminarist, the Chevalier des Grieux, and they elope. Their common joy is destroyed when Lescaut brings the wealthy Monsieur G. M. who buys Manon with jewels, furs and the promise of luxury. Des Grieux is distraught.

In the second act we see Manon as a worldly and successful woman but she cannot forget Des Grieux who dogs her presence at an opulent reception given in a house of pleasure. Manon urges Des Grieux to cheat at cards so that they may win sufficient money to go away together. The trick is discovered and in consequence Lescaut is shot dead and Manon deported as a common prostitute.

In the last act we see her arrive in Louisiana from a ship that has brought a cargo of deported whores to the New World. Manon is a ghost of her former self but Des Grieux still loves her and looks after her. He kills the prison governor who has made love to Manon and they flee to the swamplands where Manon dies.

Mayerling

The tragedy at Mayerling in 1889, when the heir to the Austro-Hungarian Empire, Crown Prince Rudolf, shot his mistress Mary Vetsera and then committed suicide, has become very popular as a late Romantic enigma. Kenneth MacMillan's ballet, first produced by the Royal Ballet in 1978 with music by Liszt and design by Georgiadis, attempts to show some of the harrowing facts of Rudolf's story.

In the first act we see Rudolf at the time of his wedding to Princess Stephanie of Belgium, flirting with his former mistress the Countess Larisch, and desperately unhappy because his mother, the Empress Elisabeth, fails to understand him, and finally terrorising his new bride on their wedding night.

In the second act, Rudolf is first shown visiting a tavern where another of his mistresses appears, surrounded by a group of Hungarian officers who have enlisted Rudolf's support in political intrigue. Countess Larisch introduces the young Mary Vetsera to him, and we see Mary at her home already obsessed with Rudolf. Rudolf's unhappiness with his family is stressed in a party scene in the Royal Palace and the act ends with Mary's arrival in Rudolf's apartment where she becomes the embodiment of his erotic dreams, sharing his obsession with death.

Act III begins with a winter scene of a Royal Hunt at which Rudolf accidentally fires at the Emperor Franz Josef and kills a member of his entourage. Rudolf now relies upon morphine; in the final scene Mary is brought to him at the hunting lodge at Mayerling, and the diseased and shattered Rudolf decides that he and Mary must die together.

Besides telling the story of Mary and Rudolf, the ballet *Mayerling* offers a dramatically vivid picture of the Hapsburg court and the tragic forces which destroy the young prince.

A Month in the Country

Frederick Ashton saw Turgenev's play in London before the Second World War. He eventually was able to make a ballet which brought some of the central themes to the dance stage in 1976 at Covent Garden when he found in Lynn Seymour a dance artist of mature beauty able to take the central role of Natalya Petrovna. The music is an arrangement of three works by Chopin for piano and orchestra. The scenery and costumes were designed by Julia Trevelyan Oman.

Natalya is a woman bored and approaching middle life. She flirts with her faithful companion Rakitin without disturbing her relationship with her husband, but it is the arrival of her young son Kolya's tutor, Belyayev, which brings tragedy to the country house where the family is spending the summer. Natalia is attracted to Belyayev. She is mortified to discover that her ward Vera is also in love with this young man and her jealousy of the girl bursts out and destroys the loving relationship between her and Vera. The fact that Belyayev suddenly reveals the depths of his love for Natalya precipitates a sad *dénouement* in which Rakitin persuades the young man to leave the house and goes with him. Natalya is left alone.

Napoli

This joyous ballet was created by August Bournonville for his Royal Danish Ballet in Copenhagen in 1842.

Its action was inspired by Bournonville's visit to Naples and tells of a young fisherman, Gennaro, who loves Teresina. Teresina has other suitors – a macaroni vendor and a lemonade seller – but she loves Gennaro. After he has brought his catch of fish to sell, the happy pair go for a sail. A storm arises and Gennaro is brought back to shore alone in his boat. In despair he mourns the lost Teresina but a monk, Fra Ambrosio, gives him a medallion of the Virgin and tells him to go and seek for his beloved.

The second act takes place in the Blue Grotto of Capri. Sea sprites bring in the lifeless form of Teresina. Golfo, their lord, falls in love with the girl and transforms her into a sea sprite. Teresina loses all memory of earthly things and when Gennaro arrives she does not recognise him. But the medallion of the Virgin overcomes Golfo's enchantments and he finally allows Teresina to be reunited with Gennaro and loads them with treasure before sending them back to Naples.

In Act III, pilgrims come to a shrine. They are amazed to see Teresina and Gennaro. Amid a brilliant display of Tarantella dancing the couple are united.

Napoli is a sunny masterpiece and its final act, which is a firework display of ebullient humour and dances, is sometimes given on its own as a sparkling divertissement. The music, chosen from several popular composers of the day, is light but charming and adds much to the infectious gaiety of the piece.

The Nutcracker

This was Tchaikovsky's last ballet score. The ballet was staged in 1892 in St Petersburg, planned by Petipa but choreographed by Lev Ivanov because of the elder ballet-master's illness.

The story is flimsy. In Act I we see a children's party at the house of Councillor Stahlbaum, whose young son and daughter, Fritz and Clara, are given presents by the mysterious but benign visitor, Drosselmeyer. To Clara he gives a toy Nutcracker which she nurses when Fritz and his friends try to break it. The guests leave after general dancing and merriment; the family goes to bed and in the drawing room the Christmas tree glitters. Suddenly Clara returns, looking for her Nutcracker toy. But as she finds it scratchings and squeakings announce that there are mice in the room. In dream-like fashion Clara watches some toy soldiers from under the Christmas tree prepare to do battle against the hordes of mice, led by their King. At the head of the toy troops is her own dear Nutcracker, and when he fights the Mouse King Clara manages to help him by throwing her slipper at the Mouse King, who falls dead. The defeated mice scuttle away and the Nutcracker – now transformed into a handsome Prince – takes Clara on a journey in a walnut-shell boat through a wintry forest where she sees the snowflakes dance.

Act II takes place in the Kingdom of Sweets where the Sugar Plum Fairy welcomes them and hears of Clara's bravery in saving the Nutcracker. A divertissement given by Tea (a Chinese dance), Coffee (an Arab dance), Chocolate (a Spanish dance), and by sugar-canes, by clowns and by Mère Gigogne and her horde of children, takes place before the culminating *pas de deux* which the Sugar Plum Fairy and the Nutcracker Prince dance in honour of Clara. A final apotheosis brings the ballet to a close.

This is the basic story of *The Nutcracker* as first staged, but the feebleness of the plot would seem to doom the ballet to oblivion were it not for the greatness of Tchaikovsky's score. Because of its irresistible charm – and its darker and more melancholy beauty in such sections as the grand *pas de deux* – the score has saved the ballet. Its popularity has meant that many choreographers and producers have made versions of the piece. They are variously successful, but as a Christmas entertainment *The Nutcracker* is now a seasonal fixture throughout the world, as well known as mince pies. It succeeds best when it stays closest to Petipa's original scenario and especially when the children in Act I are used naturally and well.

Petrushka

Often considered the most perfect of the ballets produced by the Diaghilev company because of the close collaboration between Fokine as choreographer, Stravinsky as composer, and Benois as designer, *Petrushka* is a loving portrait of the Butterweek Fair in St Petersburg in the 1840s. It was first produced in Paris in 1911.

The first scene shows the fairground and introduces the three characters – Petrushka, the Doll and the Blackamoor – who perform in the travelling theatre of an old showman. The second scene shows us Petrushka's cell where the poor puppet mimes his terror of the showman and, when the Doll is pushed into his cell, he terrifies her by his extravagance of feeling. He finally bursts his way through the wall of his cell. The next scene, set in the Blackamoor's cell, shows this witless creature first worshipping a coconut, then dancing with the feather-brained ballerina who has now been introduced into his domain. Petrushka bursts in but is ignominiously booted out by the Blackamoor.

In the final scene the carnival is at its height, with coachmen and nurses dancing amid the bustle. Suddenly the noise is quietened by a disturbance within the theatre and Petrushka rushes out pursued by the Blackamoor and followed by the Doll. The Blackamoor kills Petrushka with his scimitar and he and the Doll creep away. The crowd gather round the dying figure of Petrushka who mouths his grief. The old showman is summoned and points out that it is only a puppet of straw. The crowd disperses and as the showman drags the limp figure of the puppet away through the falling snow, Petrushka's ghost appears on the roof of the theatre miming his defiance and then collapsing as the curtain falls.

Prince Igor

The Polovtsian Dances from the opera *Prince Igor*.

For the first Russian season in Paris under the leadership of Diaghilev in 1909, Mikhail Fokine provided the choreography for the Polovtsian scene from Borodin's *Prince Igor*, which was part of the operatic offering of the season.

The action is no more than a display of fierce dancing by the warriors and women of the Polovtsy tribe, with the appearance of some captive Persian beauties, but the passion and bravura and raw, virile energy of the men (led by the great character dancer, Adolph Bolm) in 1909 created a huge sensation at the Paris première – male dancing, for too long a tasteless and effete posturing, was reborn in the West.

The Rake's Progress

Ninette de Valois took many of the themes for her ballets from English literature and painting. *The Rake's Progress* brings the world of William Hogarth's series of paintings (housed in the Sir John Soane Museum in Lincoln's Inn Fields) to vivid theatrical life. To a brilliantly effective score by Gavin Gordon, she tells the story of the Rake in six scenes.

We see the Rake with various hangers-on after he has inherited a fortune; we also see him rejecting a girl whom he has betrayed. We follow his downward progress to a brothel and a gaming house, whose degradations are contrasted with the purity and faithfulness of the betrayed girl, who still loves him. After losing his fortune in a gaming house, the Rake is flung into Bedlam where the girl visits him and sees him die at her feet.

A strongly-made dramatic work, *The Rake's Progress* was created in 1935 at Sadler's Wells Theatre with Walter Gore and Alicia Markova in the leading roles. Among its enduring qualities is the excellence of the designs by Rex Whistler, one of the finest artists of his generation, and an inspired re-creator here of eighteenth-century London.

Raymonda

First produced at the Maryinsky Theatre in St Petersburg in 1898, *Raymonda* was notable as the first ballet score by Alexander Glazunov – the true heir to Tchaikovsky as a composer of theatre music – and the 80-year-old Petipa's last successful full-length ballet. And all this despite a narrative of exceptional foolishness.

The ballet is set in mediaeval Provence. In the first act we see Raymonda awaiting the return of her beloved, Jean de Brienne, from the Crusades. A Saracen, Abdérâme, arrives to pay court to Raymonda but she rejects his advances. In a dream she seems to see a vision of Jean, who dances with her, but suddenly Abdérâme appears in her imagination and his passion frightens her so that she faints.

In the second act, guests appear at the castle where Raymonda lives, awaiting the return of Jean de Brienne. Abdérâme enters with a retinue which includes Spanish and Moorish dancers and, as they entertain the guests, Abdérâme tries to abduct Raymonda. At this moment Jean appears, with King Andrew II of Hungary, with whom he has been during the Crusade. Jean rescues Raymonda, and fights and kills Abdérâme. King Andrew unites Jean and Raymonda.

The third act shows Raymonda and Jean and their guests in a brilliant Hungarian divertissement to celebrate the wedding of the happy pair.

Still preserved in Russia, *Raymonda* has been much edited in an attempt to make some sense of its plot, while preserving the beauties of the Glazunov score. In the West in recent years Rudolf Nureyev has made stagings of the ballet which have sought to make its action more rational.

Romeo and Juliet

Shakespeare's play has always had a fascination for choreographers but it was the composition of the Prokofiev score in the 1930s which brought the story of the two lovers of Verona to the international repertory. There are many different productions which use the Prokofiev score and they all follow something of the same basic outline established by Prokofiev.

In the first act we see the feuding between the Montague and Capulet factions in Verona with the Montague Romeo and his two friends, Mercutio and Benvolio, set against Tybalt, one of the leaders of the Capulets. Romeo and his friends gatecrash the Capulet ball and there Romeo sees Juliet for the first time and the act ends with the ecstasies of the balcony scene.

In the second act Romeo and Juliet marry secretly, and amid the brawling of the Verona streets Tybalt kills Mercutio and Romeo avenges his friend by killing Tybalt.

Act III begins with the young lovers having to part as dawn breaks after their wedding night. Juliet's parents insist that she marries Count Paris. Juliet asks her nurse's assistance but her parents insist that the marriage go forward. Juliet now rushes to Friar Laurence, who had performed her marriage ceremony, and begs for his help. He gives her a potion which will bring a deathlike sleep and he will tell Romeo to rescue her from the Capulet vault. Juliet returns home and takes the potion so that when her parents enter on the morning of her marriage to Paris she seems dead. A final scene finds her in the Capulet family vault. Romeo appears, ignorant of all that has happened, and, believing Juliet dead, he kills Paris and then takes poison. Juliet awakes, discovers Romeo's corpse and stabs herself with his dagger.

Le Sacre du Printemps (The Rite of Spring)

First produced by the Diaghilev Ballet in Paris in 1913 with choreography by Nijinsky. Stravinsky's great score celebrated the extraordinary moment when the frozen Russian earth cracks and comes to life after the winter.

Conceived by Stravinsky and Nijinsky as a primitive ritual in ancient Russia, the ballet showed a tribe choosing a maiden who dances herself to death to guarantee the fruitfulness of the earth in the coming year. The ballet and its score created a celebrated riot at its first performance and Nijinsky's version only had seven performances. Many choreographers have produced versions subsequently which follow the basic plot, notably, in recent years, MacMillan, Béjart, Tetley, Bausch, Richard Alston (to the two-piano version of the score). Paul Taylor, the American contemporary dance creator, used this same two-piano score for a brilliantly effective gangster version in 1980.

Schéhérezade

Choreography by Mikhail Fokine, décor and costumes by Bakst, music by Rimsky-Korsakov

First produced by the Diaghilev Ballet in Paris in 1910, this Oriental fantasy created a sensation both in the impact of its luscious colour scheme and in the daring of its action. It is inspired by the Arabian Nights tales and is set in a harem. The Shah and his brother decide to go hunting, and in their absence the women of the harem bribe the Chief Eunuch to open the doors to the male slaves' quarters. Zobeide, the Shah's favourite, insists that one particular slave – the Golden Slave – shall be released. An orgy ensues but the Shah returns. His attendants massacre women and slaves, sparing only Zobeide until the Shah's brother indicates the corpse of the Golden Slave. The proud Zobeide knows she is doomed. She appeals once more to the Shah, then seizes a dagger and kills herself.

The Sleeping Beauty

Inspired by the world of Charles Perrault's fairy tales, *The Sleeping Beauty* remains the supreme achievement of Marius Petipa as choreographer, of Tchaikovsky as composer, and of the Imperial Ballet in St Petersburg as the culmination of nineteenth-century classic dance.

The Prologue shows the christening of the infant Princess Aurora, with fairies arriving as guests with gifts for the child and the uninvited Fairy Carabosse bursting into the palace with the curse that Aurora shall grow up and prick her finger and die. This spell is mitigated by the Lilac Fairy, Aurora's chief godmother, who had not yet bestowed her gift. She announces that Aurora shall not die, but sleep for one hundred years, to be awakened by a Prince's kiss.

Act I is set in the palace garden. Aurora has grown to beauty and at her twentieth birthday party meets the four princes who have come as suitors for her hand. She dances with them – accepting the roses they offer (the celebrated Rose Adagio) – and then receives another gift from a mysterious figure who suddenly appears. The gift is a spindle, sharply pointed. Aurora has never seen one before, because her father has banned all pointed objects from his kingdom lest Aurora shall prick her finger. This she does. She dances in a frenzy, then collapses, and the mysterious figure is revealed as Carabosse who exults that her curse has come true. As she rejoices, the Lilac Fairy also appears and casts a spell of sleep on the court. She causes a forest to grow up and hide the castle and its inhabitants.

One hundred years later, in Act II, we see Prince Florimund hunting near this same forest. He dismisses his attendants and the Lilac Fairy – who is his godmother – shows him a vision of Aurora. Florimund is enchanted and asks to be led to the palace where this beauty is sleeping. Guided by the Lilac Fairy he enters the cobwebby, mysterious palace, finds Aurora and awakens her with a kiss. As the spell of sleep ends, the whole court returns to life and Florimund and Aurora are affianced.

In Act III, fairy-tale characters come to join the court in celebration of Aurora and Florimund's wedding, an occasion for a brilliant dance divertissement which includes the dazzling Blue Bird *pas de deux,* dances for other characters, like Puss in Boots and the White Cat, and a culminating *pas de deux* for the radiant Aurora and Florimund. At the end the Lilac Fairy and attendant fairies return to bless the union.

Spartacus

The first version of *Spartacus* by the Soviet choreographer Leonid Jacobsen was not a success, and it was not until Yury Grigorovich re-studied the score, by Aram Khachaturian, with the composer, that the dramatic action was fully realised; in 1968 this new version was staged in Moscow and was recognised as a tremendously effective display of the Bolshoy Ballet's style and aspirations under Grigorovich as director.

The story is set in ancient Rome and Grigorovich's procedure is to contrast massive action-packed scenes with what he calls 'monologues' in which the four leading characters reveal their feelings. These characters are Spartacus, a Thracian slave, and his wife Phrygia; the corrupt and tyrannical Roman general Crassus and his mistress, the evil Aegina.

In the first act we see Spartacus and Phrygia sold into slavery and Spartacus inspiring his fellow slaves to revolt while Crassus and his companions indulge in an orgy. In the second act the slaves' revolt seems successful as they attack Crassus in his villa. But the third act shows the downfall of the slaves' rebellion brought about by the wavering of the slave leaders and the machinations of Aegina. At the end the slaves are defeated and Phrygia mourns over the corpse of Spartacus.

Entirely suitable in its ideology as a Soviet ballet, with its theme of a people's revolt against oppression, *Spartacus* is not unlike a Cecil B. de Mille spectacular in its cheap emotions and block-busting effects. Nevertheless, when danced by the Bolshoy's greatest artists it can hold a Western audience.

Swan Lake

Originally staged in Moscow in 1877, *Swan Lake* was given
the successful staging that launched it upon the world as the
most popular and best known of all ballets in St Petersburg in
1895, with choreography by Marius Petipa and his assistant,
Lev Ivanov. Tchaikovsky's first ballet score has done much to
ensure the ballet's continuing popularity.

The action takes place in mediaeval Germany and the first act
presents us with the young prince, Siegfried, who has come of
age and is expected by his mother to make a properly dynastic
marriage. Amid the celebrations of his birthday, Siegfried
seems moody and as the act ends he leaves with courtiers to
hunt swans.

The second act takes place by a lake side. Siegfried and his
huntsmen appear and Siegfried asks to be left alone.
Suddenly, he sees a flight of swans led by a Swan Queen. He
is amazed when the Swan Queen assumes human form. He
approaches her, calms her initial terror, and she then tells him
that she is Odette and, like her companions, is the victim of a
spell cast by the evil magician von Rothbart. By day they have
to assume the form of swans; only at nightfall can they return
to human shape. The spell can be broken only if a man swears
to love her and to be eternally faithful. Siegfried swears this
and is menaced by von Rothbart who appears in the form of a
malignant owl. Siegfried's companions are astounded when
they return and see the swan maidens and are only prevented
from shooting them when Siegfried appears. Siegfried and
Odette dance a great duet celebrating their new-found love.
The swan maidens dance but as dawn approaches they have
to fly away leaving Siegfried amazed and enraptured.

The third act takes place in the ballroom of Siegfried's palace
where guests arrive, including a group of young princesses
from among whom Siegfried's mother hopes her son will
choose a bride. Siegfried is obsessed with memories of Odette
and rejects each of these prospective fiancées. As he does so,
trumpets announce the arrival of further guests. These are a
mysterious nobleman and his daughter, and we know that

they are von Rothbart in human form and his daughter Odile, whom he has disguised exactly to resemble Odette. Siegfried, amazed and delighted, is completely deceived by Odile. Exultantly he dances with her – the celebrated Black Swan *pas de deux* – and announces that he wishes to marry her. Von Rothbart makes him swear that he will be faithful to Odile – and as Siegfried swears von Rothbart and Odile mock him and the grieving figure of Odette is seen at a window of the ballroom. Siegfried rushes out in search of her as the curtain falls.

The fourth act takes place at the lake side. The sorrowful Odette is surrounded by her swan maidens who prevent her from flinging herself to death in the lake. Siegfried appears, to beg forgiveness, and he and Odette determine to cast themselves into the lake and thus escape von Rothbart's enchantment. As they do so, von Rothbart struggles for possession of Odette but Siegfried and Odette defy him and leap into the lake. By their death they break von Rothbart's spell and the enchanter dies. The swan maidens see a vision of Odette and Siegfried reunited in a world of eternal happiness.

From the moment of its successful St Petersburg staging in 1895 *Swan Lake* became popular and has proved so – increasingly so, it must seem – ever since. Odette/Odile is a double role that is one of the supreme challenges for a classical ballerina. There have been many different versions in recent years, usually variations on the scenario and the action to give a more prominent dancing role to the male dancer. The action described above follows the 1895 staging.

La Sylphide

Choreographed in 1832 by Filippo Taglioni for his daughter Marie, with music by Schneitzhoeffer and designs by Ciceri.

This first Romantic ballet tells the story of James, a Scots crofter, with whom a sylphide (a sprite of the air) has fallen in love. James is due to be married to his fiancée Effie, but the sylphide contrives to lure the enraptured James away from his house in Act I, leaving Effie deserted.

In Act II the sylphide leads James to a glen in the mountains and she and her sister sylphs dance with him. But James had earlier offended an old witch, Madge. She tricks him into accepting a scarf which she has prepared, telling him that it will 'make the sylphide his for ever'. The scarf is poisoned. James winds it round the sylphide's shoulders, her wings drop to the ground and she dies. She is carried away by the grieving sylphs. James is distraught, and then in the distance sees his earthly beloved, Effie, going to her wedding with his rival. Madge next shows him the sylphide's body being floated heaven-ward by her companions. Her revenge is complete and James collapses and dies at her feet.

August Bournonville made his version of *La Sylphide*, with a new score by Løvenskjøld and new designs, for the Royal Danish Ballet in 1836 as a ballet to star his brilliant young pupil, Lucile Grahn, in the title role. He danced James himself. It is this version which has survived in Copenhagen until today and has in recent years been reproduced all over the world.

Les Sylphides

Mikhail Fokine created this suite of plotless dances to Chopin music as an evocation of the gentler, more lyrical Romantic style of dance which he thought had been forgotten in St Petersburg, driven out by the brilliant technical feats so adored by the balletomanes. First staged under the title *Chopiniana* in 1908 in St Petersburg, the ballet was renamed *Les Sylphides* (in memory of Marie Taglioni and *La Sylphide*, whose style is part of the ballet's inspiration) by Serge Diaghilev when it formed part of the first season of Russian ballet and opera in Paris in 1909.

The ballet uses a company of female soloists with one male
dancer. The action is plotless – a romantic rêverie. It was
Diaghilev's favourite ballet and is now danced throughout the
world.

The Two Pigeons

In 1961 Frederick Ashton made his own version of this ballet,
using the score by Messager that had been originally
composed for the Paris Opéra in 1886.

Ashton's version, made for the Sadler's Wells Royal Ballet,
shows a young artist in his Paris studio exasperated by the
antics of his model, a young girl deeply in love with him. A
troupe of gypsies arrive and the young artist falls for the wiles
of a beautiful gypsy girl and he follows her away, leaving his
beloved disconsolate.

In the second act the artist is enjoying the gypsy life but the
gypsy girl has only been amusing herself with him and the
young artist is eventually beaten up by the gypsies.
Chastened, he makes his way home to his true love.

technical terms used in ballet

Arabesque The dancer's body is supported on one leg while the other is extended behind and the arms are usually placed in a complementary line following the stretch of the body. There are several forms of arabesque; the entrance of the Shades in *La Bayadère* shows the corps de ballet of girls making their entrance in a succession of *arabesques penchées* (deeply inclined arabesque).

Attitude A pose in which the dancer stands on one leg, the other raised behind and bent at the knee in a position supposedly derived from Giovanni da Bologna's statue of Mercury. The working leg may also be held in a comparable position in front of the body – an attitude *devant*. In the Rose Adagio from the first act of *The Sleeping Beauty* Aurora stands in attitude and holds her balance. At the end of the sequence she extends her working leg into an exultant arabesque.

Ballabile An Italian term which in the nineteenth century was used to describe the group dances by the corps de ballet: examples are the dances for the Wilis in *Giselle* Act II or the Sylphides in

La Sylphide Act II or for the Shades in the Kingdom of Shades from *La Bayadère* and the nymphs in the Vision Scene of *The Sleeping Beauty*.

Ballerina

A title traditionally bestowed upon the principal female dancers of a company. In Russia it was an official ranking in Tsarist times and it still should be used only to denote those dancers who undertake and sustain the great classical roles. Though the popular press may refer to any little dancer who hits the headlines as a 'ballerina', the ballet public knows that there are very few ballerinas in the world. The leading ballerina of a company is the *prima ballerina*. Only the most exalted of the great star dancers can justify the title *prima ballerina assoluta*, which was an official ranking bestowed on only two dancers in Imperial Russia, Pierina Legnani and Mathilde Kshessinskaya. The memorial tablet in St Paul's Church, Covent Garden, is incorrect in describing the glorious Tamara Karsavina as an *assoluta*. In recent times the accolade has been officially given to Maya Plisetskaya and Margot Fonteyn.

Ballet d'action

This is a term used to describe the form of dramatic narrative dance which emerged in the mid-eighteenth century and is associated with the writings of John Weaver and Jean Georges Noverre.

Balletomane

A ballet lover who became addicted to the ballet in Imperial Russia became identified as a balletomane. In 1934 Arnold Haskell published *Balletomania*, a best-selling and immensely rewarding study of ballet going and ballet history, which introduced the word into the English language, and which we would urge everyone to read.

Ballets Russes

Under this general term can be grouped all the troupes of dancers who followed in the trail of the Diaghilev Ballet Russe company. The implication is of émigré Russians trying to continue the Diaghilev enterprise. To understand the various struggles for power and changes of identity in the several Ballet Russe companies we refer you to G. B. L. Wilson's *Dictionary of Ballet*.

Ballon The quality of springing and bouncing movement in any jumping steps which derives from correct training of the feet.

Barre The wooden rail which surrounds a dance studio at waist height, used by the dancer to find and sustain balance. It is not a prop; the dancer's hand rests but lightly on the barre during the first part of a class.

Battement A beating movement of the leg which can have various forms. At the end of the adagio in *Swan Lake* Act II Odette performs a series of *petits battements,* tiny beats against her ankle, as she turns in a supported pirouette. In class, *grands battements* require the dancer to throw the leg forward, sideways and backwards to the highest possible extension

Batterie A succession of beaten steps in which the feet beat or cross in the air. In *The Sleeping Beauty* last act the Blue Bird crosses the stage in a diagonal of *brisés volés* which are steps of *batterie.*

Bourrée The *pas de bourrée* is a series of small steps which, performed by a dancer on pointe, gives an impression of swift gliding over the stage. The Queen of the Wilis in *Giselle* Act II performs these steps in her first entry and Fokine's *The Swan* is built entirely upon this step.

Character dancing This description is used for the performance of national dances and roles which are largely comprised of dramatic or comic mime. Examples of the former are the national dances in the ballroom act of *Swan Lake,* and of the latter many of the roles to be found in such Massine ballets as *La Boutique Fantasque* and Ashton's *La Fille mal gardée* (Widow Simone) and *Cinderella* (the Ugly Sisters). See also *demi-caractère.*

Coda The tradition grand *pas de deux* in a ballet comprises four sections: and opening *adage* in which the male dancer supports and shows off the ballerina; a *variation* for the man; a *variation* for the ballerina; and the *coda* in which both dancers indulge in the most brilliant feats of virtuosity. The coda to the Black Swan *pas de deux* in Act III of *Swan Lake* contains soaring leaps and pirouettes for the man and the famous (and infamous) 32 *fouettés* for the ballerina.

191

Corps de ballet

The corps de ballet is the bedrock of a classical ballet company. In the nineteenth-century repertory the dancers are shown off in the big sequences in which they provide support for the central characters – the Shades in *La Bayadère*, the Wilis in *Giselle* Act II, the swans in *Swan Lake.* In contemporary ballets the corps can be seen at its best in such different styles as the stars in Ashton's *Cinderella*, the supporting artists in many Balanchine ballets, or the highly dramatic crowd performers in MacMillan's *Romeo and Juliet* and *Mayerling.* The corps de ballet, more than any star performer, reflects a company's style, schooling and importance. A good corps de ballet is the product of many years' hard training by teachers and *répétiteurs* as well as by the dancers themselves. It is easy to sign up a group of 'Stars of the Ballet'; there is no such thing as an 'instant' corps de ballet.

Danseur noble

The prince in the traditional nineteenth-century roles offers the best image of the *danseur noble.* He must possess sound classical training, nobility of presence and elegance of physique. Curiously, despite the passage of two hundred years, the qualities required of the dancer in the noble style of the eighteenth century still really apply to the *danseur noble* of today. The supreme example in the post-war years was the Danish star Erik Bruhn.

Demi-caractère

Character dancing which yet remains within the disciplines of the classic style is called *demi-caractère.* Such roles as Captain Belaye in *Pineapple Poll*, the Jester in *Cinderella*, Puck in *The Dream*, are typical examples. Roles written for brilliant technical dancers who do not have the physical stature for noble roles are often *demi-caractère* parts.

Divertisse-ment

Any assemblage of assorted dance numbers can pass as a divertissement. In the old nineteenth-century ballets there was usually a divertissement in which various examples of character dancing were on display to titillate the audience's appetite. Today a ballet which comprises a string of plotless dances may sometimes be called a divertissement. But basically a divertissement is an entertainment within a ballet and the final acts of *Coppélia* and *The Sleeping Beauty* are fine examples.

Double work
(See also **pas de deux** and **partnering**)
The term is used for all dances in which one dancer is supported, lifted or presented by another. Usually, the male dancer has the responsibility of steering the ballerina through a *pas de deux*, making all her technical feats seem effortless and showing no strain at all in his own movements. A good partner is prized above all else by a ballerina; he will understand and anticipate the ballerina's every action and mood. Great partnerships establish a kind of emotional sympathy and the pair are seen to move as one. Celebrated partnerships have included those of Markova and Dolin; Haydee and Cragun; Sibley and Dowell; Farrell and Martins. Male dancers such as Donald MacLeary, Ivan Nagy and Desmond Kelly have earned much justified praise for the skill and nobility of their partnering.

Elevation
The ability to soar high in the air is described as elevation. It refers to the actual jumping power of a dancer's muscles. It is a quality very different from the elasticity of *ballon* (q.v.)

Enchaîne-ment
Literally a linking, this French term signifies the combination of steps in a phrase, either in a ballet or in a class where the teacher will invent sequences of steps to stretch and interest the pupils.

Entrechat
A vertical jump, always from fifth position, in which the legs and feet criss-cross at the lower calf. The *entrechats* are numbered according to the positions that the feet take during the course of the movement. Thus two changes is an *entrechat quatre*, three makes for an *entrechat six*. Exceptional dancers can perform *entrechat dix*.

Épaulement
Literally 'shouldering', *épaulement* conveys the altering of the positions of the shoulders in relation to the head and the rest of the trunk which gives nuance and variety to positions. It is an essential quality in the artistry of the dancer.

193

Fouetté   A whipped turn on one foot in which the working leg is
extended to the side and then brought in to the knee as the
body revolves. The step is usually performed by the ballerina
on pointe in multiples, for example, Odile and her 32 *fouettés*
in *Swan Lake* Act III, but it can be performed by a man on
three quarter toe – John Gilpin produced prodigies of *fouettés*
in *Etudes.*

Jeté   Any jump which moves from one foot to another is a *jeté*. The
leg is thrown forward, hence the use of the French term *jeter*,
to throw, but the *jeté* can be forwards, backwards or sideways,
large or small, in a single direction or turning.

Leotard   The one-piece all-over suit worn by dancers was invented and
named after Jules Léotard, a French trapeze artist (1830–70).
With the invention of stretch fabrics the leotard has become a
cliché of much modern choreography and the shining artificial
fabric can sometimes make the cast of a ballet look like so
many sardines.

Line   The harmonious placing of the body in any position, notably
in the long extensions of an arabesque, suggest the quality of
good 'line' so necessary to fine dancing.

Mime   The traditional gestures by which emotions or actions are
indicated is known as mime or pantomime. This sign
language has its roots in the work of the Italian commedia
dell' arte and it became strictly codified in the
nineteenth-century repertory where a set sequence of
gestures was used to explain certain narrative points. But the
audience was required to understand this language,
otherwise such scenes as Odette's explanation to Siegfried of
her plight in *Swan Lake* Act II would be incomprehensible.
Some mime gestures are entirely clear – though we would
observe that the order of expression follows that of the French
language, hence the hero will 'say' to the heroine 'I you
love/Je vous aime' – but others are irrational as, for example,
the rotating of the hands above the head to suggest 'dance'.
Today traditional mime is often removed from the old ballets –
which is a mistake.

194

Notation	The need to write down the steps and movements of a dance are as old as theatre dance itself in the West. Systems have emerged from the very earliest fifteenth-century example of words and letters to denote movement. By the beginning of the eighteenth century systems of 'choreography' (the original and correct meaning of this word being the writing down of dance) had been devised and published to show the track along the ground which dancers had to follow. In the nineteenth century further and more complex systems were invented, sometimes using stick figures. In the twentieth century the two best-known systems are those produced by Rudolf von Laban – Labanotation – and Rudolf Benesh, Benesh notation or Choreology. Both of these are widely used and provide an accurate system of writing down the movement of the human body. Today many ballet companies employ a dance notator to record their repertories as an adjunct to filmed and video records of works.
Pas	A step. All steps in ballet are known as *pas*. There are uses of the word in which the quality of the movement is implicit, for example, *pas de chat* which emulates the little pouncing jump of a cat, and others in which the actual number of participants is indicated, such as *pas de deux, pas de trois, pas de quatre,* etc. In other uses the nature of the choreography is indicated as in the *pas de l'ombre*, the shadow dance from *Ondine, pas des rubans*, a ribbon dance, and also in the idea of a *pas d'action* which implies a narrative sequence of choreography.
Pirouette	A complete revolution of the body performed on one leg.
Placing	The natural and harmonious disposition of the body without distortion is implied in the idea of good placing. This quality is essential for good balance in any movement as the dancer must have total command of the distribution of the body's weight.
Plié	The first exercise performed in class is a *plié*, the bending of the legs in correct alignment over the turned out feet and with the torso held erect. This fundamental movement in ballet

brings the body gradually into action and strength of *plié* will
provide both the springboard and then the cushion for all
jumping movements. (From the French verb *plier*, to bend.)

Pointe work Dancing on the tips of the toes in the classic academic dance
was a development of female technique during the nineteenth
century. Comments as early as 1813 describe a dancer at the
Paris Opéra on the very tips of her toes. It was Marie Taglioni
who gave an aesthetic and dramatic validity to pointe work as
an image of weightless flight and gentle hovering above the
ground. Others of the ballerinas in the Romantic age used this
technical feat to suggest brilliance or to reveal their virtuosity
and they danced in soft shoes, their toes protected by cotton
wadding and some stitching round the edge of the shoe.
Gradually a stronger and blocked shoe was evolved by Italian
shoemakers to enable the ballerinas of the middle of the
century to perform increasingly brilliant feats but the
generality of corps de ballet dancers did not go on pointe until
later in the century. By the end of the nineteenth century
every female dancer was expected to be expert in pointe
work. In ballet class the final section for the girls always
involves extensive pointe work.

Port de bras Literally the carriage of the arms, the term conveys both the
accepted five positions of the arms (which differ according to
the method of training, the 'school') and the use of the arms as
part of the total dance image of the body. Beautiful and freely
moving arms are essential to good dancing.

Positions There are five positions of the feet in classical ballet, a way of
placing the feet and legs which was already established by
the end of the seventeenth century. They depend upon
turn-out (q.v.).

**Rake of the
stage** Most stages slope down towards the proscenium arch and
dancers have to take into consideration the way they work
upon this incline – gentle or steep – when they are performing
in different theatres, because it will affect their balance. In
some theatres, the Paris Opéra an example, the rehearsal

room will have a floor which matches exactly the incline of the stage so that dancers are permanently accustomed to the same rake.

Régisseur   The person responsible for the rehearsing and presentation of repertory ballets. Sometimes known as a *répétiteur*, literally the man who rehearses ballets. A régisseur usually has over-all responsibility for the productions in all their aspects. This function Serge Grigoriev fulfilled for the entire twenty years of the Diaghilev Ballet. The *répétiteur* is responsible for making sure that the cast of a ballet knows the steps and the style of the ballet.

Rosin   The solid left behind when the oil has been extracted from crude turpentine. Dancers always rub the soles of their shoes in the rosin box which is found in the wings of a theatre before going on stage to prevent slipping. Rosin may also sometimes be sprinkled on an especially slippery and treacherous stage to help prevent falls and accidents.

'School'   The convenient term to identify the technical and aesthetic approach of a particular method of classical ballet training and performance. Basically all 'schools' work towards the same end, but we can talk of the qualities of the Bournonville 'School', the lyricism of the English 'School', or the magnificent use of the back associated with the Vaganova 'School' in Russia.

Tour en l'air   A turn in the air usually, though not always, executed by male dancers. The body is held erect and the dancer performs one or two turns in the air and lands in the fifth position (a fact more honoured, alas, in the breach than in the observance). Rarely, a male dancer will perform triple *tours*. Richard Cragun in *The Taming of the Shrew* is the most brilliant example in our time. Female dancers are rarely called upon to do this step, but Markova alway finished the Polka in *Façade* with a double *tour en l'air*. No dancer since has been able to.

Travesti   When dancers appear in costuming of the opposite sex they are said to be *en travesti*. The debased French ballet of the

197

late nineteenth century showed the hero of *Coppélia* and *Les Deux Pigeons* played by a pretty girl *en travesti,* and this tradition lasted with *Coppélia* at the Paris Opéra into the 1950s when Paulette Dynalix was the last female Franz. Male travesty playing ranges from the appearance of Enrico Cecchetti as the mother in *La Fille mal gardée* to the Ugly Sisters in Ashton's *Cinderella* (played in the English pantomime tradition).

Turn-out The execution of any ballet step depends upon the first principle of the academic style, the turn-out of the leg from the hip to an angle of 90 degrees. See Chapter 5.

Tutu The long mid-calf and floating tarlatans of the Sylphide in 1832 gradually became shortened as the nineteenth century progressed and female virtuosity demanded that the audience see the ballerina's legs working. Such virtuoso ballerinas as Virginia Zucchi shortened their skirts to the knee and this tutu became the accepted ballerina costume for the next fifty years. By the 1930s the tutu had become even more abbreviated and stiffened.

Variation A solo dance, e.g. the fairies' solos in the Prologue of *The Sleeping Beauty.*

recommended further reading

Listed below are a few of the many books available about ballet. Though not all are currently in print, they should be available from libraries or may be sought out in second-hand bookstores.

history

Movement and Metaphor, Lincoln Kirstein. Pitman
An excellent survey of the component parts of ballet, and of fifty seminal ballets from the Renaissance onwards. Superbly illustrated.

The Dancer's Heritage, Ivor Guest. The Dancing Times
A concise history of ballet which is the standard textbook for the GCE O-Level Ballet examination.

Ballet: An Illustrated History, Mary Clarke and Clement Crisp. A & C Black
The history is told both through the text and in the many informative captions to the illustrations.

A History of Ballet and Dance, Alexander Bland. Barry & Jenkins
A very well illustrated survey of the whole field of ballet.

The History of Dance, Mary Clarke and Clement Crisp. Orbis
> The origins and development of dance from ancient times until today, with 300 illustrations.

The Romantic Ballet in Paris, Ivor Guest. Pitman
> The definitive study of the period by an authority whose every book is worth reading. They include biographies of Fanny Elssler, Fanny Cerrito and Jules Perrot; also *The Romantic Ballet in London* and *The Ballet of the Second Empire*.

Era of the Russian Ballet, Natalia Roslavleva. Gollancz
> The essential history by a Soviet scholar.

The Diaghilev Ballet, S. L. Grigoriev, translated by Vera Bowen. Constable
> The history of the Ballet Russe, 1909–29 from the inside. Essential reading.

Diaghileff, Arnold Haskell and Walter Nouvel. Gollancz
> Still the best study, written by two men who knew him.

Diaghilev, Richard Buckle. Weidenfeld
> The most comprehensive study of the great man, which forms a pair with the same author's *Nijinsky*.

Early Memoirs, Bronislava Nijinska. Faber

The One and Only: The Ballet Russe de Monte Carlo,
> Jack Anderson. Dance Books

De Basil's Ballets Russes, Katherine Sorley Walker. Hutchinson
> An important and enjoyable study.

Balletomania, Arnold Haskell. Gollancz
> The history of Haskell's own obsession with ballet and one of the most infectiously enjoyable books mingling history and insights. Still fresh after fifty years.

dancers

Nijinsky Dancing, Lincoln Kirstein. Thames & Hudson
> A ravishing collection of photographs with a most illuminating commentary.

Pavlova, Keith Money. Collins
> A beautifully illustrated and magnificently researched book about the great dancer.

Giselle and I, Alicia Markova. Barry & Rockliffe
> A fascinating commentary by a great ballerina about her greatest role.

200

Ballerina: Portraits and Impressions of Nadia Nerina,
    Clement Crisp (ed). Weidenfeld
    The life of this enchanting ballerina recorded in her own words and those of her
    contemporaries.

Fonteyn: The Making of a Legend, Keith Money. Collins
    A pictorial record of a great career.

The Nureyev Image, Alexander Bland. Studio Vista.
    A very good assessment of this exceptional dancer's work and life.

Baryshnikov at Work, Charles France (ed). A & C Black
    A collection of superb photographs with an illuminating commentary on his roles
    by the great dancer.

A Dance Autobiography, Natalia Makarova. Knopf, New York
    The great ballerina discusses her life and her roles in a magnificently illustrated
    book.

Lynn Seymour. Photographs by Anthony Crickmay. Studio Vista
    A magnificent collection of photographs by the outstanding ballet photographer
    Anthony Crickmay, with a commentary by the subject about her work.

companies

Many ballet companies have produced commemorative volumes about their
work. We list here a few of the more interesting ones.

Ballet Rambert

Dancers of Mercury, Mary Clarke. A & C Black
    The story of Ballet Rambert and its founder.

Fifty Years of Ballet Rambert. London
    A souvenir book published to commemorate the company's fiftieth anniversary.

The Royal Ballet

Vic-Wells: A Ballet Progress, P. W. Manchester. Gollancz
    An affectionate and knowledgeable account of the first decade.

The Sadler's Wells Ballet: A History and an Appreciation, Mary Clarke.
    A & C Black
    The essential survey of the first twenty-five years drawn from
    eye-witness accounts.

The Royal Ballet: The First Fifty Years, Alexander Bland. Threshold Books
The story thus far with most valuable factual appendices.

The Royal Ballet: a picture history, Kathrine Sorley Walker and Sarah
Woodcock. Threshold/Corgi
An excellent guide to the company in its fiftieth year history.

Dame Ninette de Valois' own books, *Invitation to the Ballet*, *Come Dance With
Me* and *Step by Step*, throw much light on the creation of a national ballet.

USA

The New York City Ballet, Lincoln Kirstein. A & C Black
Superbly illustrated and absolutely essential, the history of the New York City Ballet
by the man who made it possible. Its text (minus the pictures) was republished in
1978 and updated as *Thirty Years of the New York City Ballet.*

Repertory in Review, Nancy Reynolds. Dial Press, New York
A complete analysis of all the repertory staged by the New York City Ballet to 1977.

American Ballet Theatre, Charles Payne. Knopf, New York
The tremendously well illustrated and fascinating inside story of the company.

design

Design For Ballet, Mary Clarke and Clement Crisp. Studio Vista
The most comprehensive survey of the subject.

Ballet Designs and Illustrations, Brian Reade. HMSO
A selection of the design riches of the Victoria & Albert Museum.

Splendour at Court, Roy Strong. Weidenfeld
A fascinating analysis of the Renaissance court entertainments, profusely illustrated.

Designing for the Dancer, Roy Strong, Ivor Guest and Richard Buckle.
Victoria & Albert Museum
A monograph by three authorities produced on the occasion of the Theatre
Museum's big ballet costume and design exhibition. It concentrates on costume.

technical

A Dictionary of Ballet Terms, Leo Kersley and Janet Sinclair. A & C Black
The best possible explanation of ballet terms for the layman, with clear line drawings
by Peter Revitt.

202

The Classic Ballet, Muriel Stuart and Lincoln Kirstein, Knopf, New York
The best analysis of the classic dance with line drawings by Carlus Dyer.

dictionaries and repertory

A Dictionary of Ballet, G. B. L. Wilson. A & C Black
This invaluable pioneer work started out as the *Penguin Dictionary of Ballet* in 1957 and is now available in much enlarged form in hardback. Not merely a reference book but an un-put-downable read.

Concise Dictionary of Ballet, Horst Koegler. OUP
A companion volume to G. B. L. Wilson, especially valuable on Russian and European entries.

The Dance Encyclopedia, Anatole Chujoy and P. W. Manchester. A. S. Barnes

The Encyclopedia of Dance and Ballet, Mary Clarke and David Vaughan, (eds). Pitman
These two volumes provide valuable articles by foremost authorities, and illustrations which offer detailed information about the world of ballet and dance.

The Complete Book of Ballets and its *Supplement*; also *Ballets Past and Present* and *Ballets of Today*, C. W. Beaumont. London
These books are basic to any ballet-goer's library, providing complete descriptions and analyses of several hundred ballets.

Balanchine's Complete Stories of the Great Ballets, George Balanchine and Francis Mason. Doubleday, New York
An arbitrary (in the length of individual entries) but fascinating volume, especially when Balanchine is commenting on his own work.

Ballet and Dance: A Guide to the Repertory, Peter Brinson and Clement Crisp. David & Charles
Published by Pan as the *Pan Book of Ballet* in London in 1981 in paperback. A guide to the contemporary repertory in Britain, Australia and Canada in which some 130 ballets are discussed.

The Balletgoer's Guide, Mary Clarke and Clement Crisp. Michael Joseph
A discussion of design and ballet's background precedes a splendidly illustrated analysis of 120 ballets with details of many different versions of such favourites as *Swan Lake* and *The Nutcracker* and an illustration of some of the basic training of the dancer.

index

Picture Credits

Baines, Christopher 147; BBC Hulton Picture Library 116; Béjart, Alain 31; British Museum, The 71; Caras, Steven 53; Clarke-Crisp Collection 45, 47, 61, 62, 64, 67, 70, 73, 77, 78, 81, 83, 91, 95, 96, 98–99, 103, 104, 119; Cockrill, Andrew 154; Crickmay, Anthony frontis, 13, 17, 23, 26, 50, 57, 106, 114, 123, 124; Davis, Frederika 14–15; Fatauros, Jorge 127; Granada Television 159; Jessel, Camilla 137; Leder, Peggy 117; London Weekend Television 21, 120; Midland Bank 36; Novosti Press Agency 48; O'Callaghan, Jas D. 131; Oxenham, Andrew 128; Robinson, Stuart 156–7; Round, Roy 41, 113; Spatt, Leslie E. 18, 19, 28, 161; Swope, Martha 6, 52, 55, 134; Theatre Museum, Victoria and Albert Museum 34, 101, 109, 151; Welch, Victor 143.